T0278392

FINDING HOME

HOW THE HOLOCAUST
SHAPED MY FAMILY

ELANA KLAUSNER VIKAN

WITH

GARY VIKAN

ILLUSTRATED BY

FREDDA BRENNAN

For Mommie and Eddy,
who bore war wounds that could not be seen.

TABLE OF CONTENTS

INTRODUCTION   1

FROM VILNA TO THE SAFETY OF FRANCE   7

FROM FRANCE TO THE SAFETY OF AMERICA   21

IMMIGRANTS ON COMMUNITY DRIVE   41

BRYN MAWR AND "NOBLENESS TO SOCIAL AIMS"   63

PARIS AND *L'ACADÉMIE* AT MAXIM'S   75

MY JOURNEY TO PONARY   95

THE SURVIVORS, THE VICTIMS   107

THE FAMILIES   149

THE TIMELINE   151

ACKNOWLEDGEMENTS   157

THE TEAM   159

INTRODUCTION

March 26, 1956: It is Passover in the Klausner household. We gather around the small table in our tiny kitchen: Mommie, Papa, Eddy, and me, 10 years old. Each of us with our own Haggadah, which we read from back to front, in Hebrew and in English.

My diary entry reads, "SPECIAL DAY: Eddy got into Harvard!" We are all feeling that not just Eddy but the whole little Klausner family, Polish-Jewish immigrants at 33 Community Drive in Cranston, Rhode Island, has finally made it in America.

We are euphoric.

At critical moments as the dramatic Exodus story unfolds, Eddy rushes to the den, with me trailing behind, to play the familiar Passover tunes on our upright piano and, with me, to sing them so loud that Mommie and Papa can hear us in the kitchen. My favorite is "Go Down Moses." I belt out "Let my people go!" at the top of my lungs.

Our kitchen is brightly lit, warm, and humid, smelling of matzah ball soup, roast chicken, and mashed potatoes. The Formica table is covered with our special-occasion white tablecloth. At its center is our large seder plate from Israel displaying symbols of the Exodus story: a shank bone (sacrifice), an egg (the circle of life), horseradish (bitterness of slavery), chopped apple and walnuts (mortar of the pyramids), and parsley in saltwater (tears). Plus, three matzahs, unleavened to recall the haste of the flight from Egypt, in a special embroidered bag with three compartments, which I still have. Eddy and I will happily eat matzah for a week, bringing pieces to school to share with friends.

In his chair at the head of the table, Papa sits on a pillow, to mark the comfort of freedom from bondage. As the youngest, I'm proud to sing the "Four Questions" in Hebrew, in response to, "Why is this night different from all other nights?" The Four Questions explain the symbolism of those odd items on the plate before us.

We follow the Haggadah text closely, trying to rush Papa so we can get to our dinner before it gets cold.

For Papa, this Passover family gathering is an opportunity to engage Eddy and me in discussing big questions about freedom, history's lessons, and our own family's story of escape from the Nazis to safety in America. This is a thrilling adventure story involving forged documents, fear of arrest, and a ship full of Jewish refugees sailing into New York Harbor. It is a sad story, because Mommie's family does not make it – they are all murdered by the Nazis. And it is a scary story. But I know the ending is a happy one, since here we are, celebrating Passover in our own kitchen – and Eddy is going to Harvard.

In my mind, the Jews escaping the Pharaoh become our little family – Mommie, Papa, and Eddy, then just a two-year-old – escaping Hitler. But there is one enormous difference: Those Jews have no intention of going back to Egypt one day, while France, despite the danger my parents had faced there, seems to me to be "home" – the place where I was supposed to have been born. I dream that our family will someday return. And I'm getting ready, since Papa is teaching me French!

Papa's Passover adventure story about the Holocaust revolves around two heroes and three dramatic scenes, all easy for me to visualize.

The heroes are Papa's uncle Gustave, who gets his friend, future President of the United States Harry Truman, to send him an entry visa for America; and Mommie's brother Kolia, who gives up his life to protect the Jewish children in his hospital.

And the three scenes of high drama? In the first, Uncle Misha stands lookout at the photo studio when Papa goes in to get his forged documents, so that if Papa is arrested, he will rush to tell Mommie and Eddy and they will go into hiding.

In the second scene, Papa confesses his deceit about the forged documents to a kind woman at the Marseille police station, but she *still* gives him the papers he needs to get our family out of France.

And in the closing scene, which seems to come straight out of a movie, Mommie, Papa, and little Eddy stand on the deck of a huge ship on a sunny June day, sailing past the Statue of Liberty with tears in their eyes.

The year, Papa says, is 1942 – three years before I was born.

Eddy went to Harvard and seven years later I went to Bryn Mawr. During my junior year I was one of six American college girls invited to go to Paris to be members of *l'Académie* at Maxim's. Emblematic of that fairy-tale adventure is the famous Maxim's Restaurant, just off the Place de la Concorde, where we lunched each Friday with the owner's wife and *Académie* director, the formidable Madame ("Maggie") Vaudable. (It was under her husband, Louis, that Maxim's became the world's most famous restaurant after World War II.) Joining us each week for lunch, at Maggie's invitation, would be a member of the Parisian cultural pantheon – from the brilliant young conductor Pierre Boulez to 80-year-old François Mauriac, who had won the Nobel Prize in Literature.

Mommie, Papa, and Eddy had sailed from France, via Casablanca, to New York City in June 1942 on the renowned Portuguese "Friendship Vessel," the S.S. *Serpa Pinto,* to begin their new life in America. I sailed from New York City to France in September 1965 on the "Fastest Ship in the World," the S.S. *United States,* to begin my junior year in Paris under the tutelage of Maxim's.

Two transatlantic crossings a generation apart; two transformative journeys. And 40 years later, there was a third journey – my journey – to the oil pits at Ponary, just south of Vilnius, Lithuania, to the spot where the Nazis murdered Mommie's family.

Could my ten-year-old mind, at Passover back in 1956, have imagined a more magical "return home" to France than *l'Académie* at Maxim's?

Could I then have dreamed that Eddy, our family's rising star, would later suffer mental collapse and die penniless in the locked geriatric ward of a nursing home?

Eddy was born one month before the beginning of World War II in a small French industrial town near the German border. For the next decade he was on the move. I was born on the first United Nations Day, October 24th, in New York, two months after the War had ended.

Eddy was a war refugee and a victim of the Holocaust. I was born an American, a first-generation survivor.

ONE

FROM VILNA TO THE SAFETY OF FRANCE

Even as an adult, I chose to believe that France was the true home country of my parents. But contrary to my personal mythology, their story began not in France but in Vilna.

Vilna – now Vilnius, in modern-day Lithuania – with its generations of Talmudic scholars, had long been the spiritual heart of Eastern European Jewry. In my parents' time, when Vilna was first part of Russia, then Poland, it had more than one hundred synagogues and religious study halls. Between the Wars, Vilna became Eastern European Jewry's cultural, intellectual, and political center. It then experienced a brief but brilliant golden age and was known as the "Jerusalem of the North."

Jewish Vilna, with more than a third of the city's population, was a city within a city, with scores of accomplished writers, poets, actors, and musicians, dozens of Jewish social and sports clubs, and Yiddish and Hebrew newspapers, journals, and publishing houses. Its Yiddish theater was renowned throughout the Jewish world. Vilna was also known for its progressive Jewish secondary schools (my father's domain) and its vibrant social life among the Jewish elite (my mother's domain).

My father, Isaac Klauzner, was born in July 1903 in Troki, a lake town 17 miles west of Vilna; the family moved to Vilna at the outbreak of World War I, when he was 11. He was next to the oldest among six children of a prosperous local accountant named Hayim (photo 1). As a child, my father had been exposed to radiation and his hair fell out; burn scars on the back of his head and neck attested to that event. I have always assumed that he had an illness associated with his neck and that (X-ray) radiation, which was then just beginning to be used medically, was part of his treatment. Since not all of his hair follicles were destroyed, for years he shaved his head.

My mother, Anna Spokoiny, was born in Vilna in December 1909. She was the youngest of four children of a successful merchant and leading rabbi named Osher, who was among the last mohels serving the city's Jewish community (photo 2). Her father also held the hereditary position of warden of the *Kloyz* (study hall) of the famous Gaon of Vilna (d. 1797), the great scholar and spiritual leader who had for generations been a source of pride for Vilna Jews.

Jewish Vilna encompassed rich and poor neighborhoods, bound by multiple charitable agencies. The narrow winding lanes of the Jewish Quarter, at the center of the city near the Great Synagogue, teemed with poor immigrants. I imagine a cacophony: the sounds of vendors hawking their wares, the rhythmic chanting of the Torah, and the shouts of heated debates. Vilna was home to a bewildering array of competing Jewish political movements. Both my parents' families were ardent Zionists, and my mother's brother Kolia was a leader of a leftist Zionist workers' movement founded as a response to the Bund, Vilna's anti-Zionist socialist party. The Bund chose Yiddish and a European future for Jews – instead of Hebrew and Eretz Israel. Walking in the streets of Vilna, my parents would have heard passersby speaking Polish, Russian, Belorussian, Yiddish, and Hebrew.

My father, a brilliant and determined student, graduated from the Sofia M. Gurevich Gymnasium at age 17. There, both Yiddish and Russian were used daily, with an emphasis on Yiddish for student work. The school shared goals espoused by the Bund; its mission included progressive teaching methods and an unusually broad curriculum. My father's diploma is a large folded document on sturdy paper, printed in a clear old Russian font, with its specifics handwritten in a carefully rendered cursive (photo 3). The head of school, ten teachers, and the secretary signed it. The subjects form a staggering list: four levels of mathematics; physics; earth sciences; history; geography; Jewish history; natural history; Hebrew literature; Russian language and literature; Polish, German, French, and Latin language; philosophy; and economics. Next to each subject is the word "excellent," followed by the top grade, the number 5. The document bears a large red wax seal and is dated June 5, 1921.

My father was proud of his high school academic record, as he would be proud of the report cards that Eddy and I brought home years later. Not only did he take his diploma with him during his long and circuitous journey to America, but he also referenced it with the phrase "all subjects: excellent" in a spare, two-page autobiography he wrote in tortured script after his near-fatal stroke in 1988.

My father's graduation photographs show a serious, focused student. With his bald head and high-collared black shirt, he has a stoic, even monastic appearance. Here and in other photos, his expression is stern, even by the standards of that era's studio photos.

My father's last name suited his academic focus, diligence, and ascetic appearance. The Jewish study halls of Vilna were called *kloyzes*. His family name, Klauzner, which became Klausner when my parents became naturalized U.S. citizens, is related to "hermit" and to "cloister," an open courtyard that connects to buildings by a covered walkway. Associated first with monastic life and then with the university, it encloses its inhabitants and protects them from distractions. (The cloister of the old library at Bryn Mawr College was a favorite spot of mine for study and thinking. Later, as a teacher, I would explain to my students that university life would offer them the possibility of a "vita contemplativa" of quiet and focused thought, in contrast to the social flurry of high school, a "vita activa.")

It is not surprising that my father chose to leave Vilna to continue his studies, given the turmoil faced at the time by the venerable local Jesuit university, where his younger brother Israel would enroll a decade later. It was shut down and reopened three times by three different governments between 1918 and 1920. My father looked instead to study at a German university, as his father's cousin, the noted Israeli historian Joseph Klausner, had a generation earlier.

My father entered the University of Karlsruhe in 1922 to study chemistry. But sensing what he called "resistance to Jews" in that German town, he moved the next year 50 miles south and across the Rhine River into France, to the University of Strasbourg. There he graduated three years later, in 1926, as an *Ingénieur-Chimiste*. He then started work on his Ph.D., which he never completed. My father once told me that he felt obliged to find a job to help support his sister Sarah in medical school. (This may explain his profound disappointment when I eventually abandoned my Ph.D. in comparative literature at Princeton.)

In 1927, my father started his first job, as chemist of the steel mill in the small French town of Villerupt, near the Luxembourg border. In 1929 he moved on to become the *Ingénieur-Chef de Laboratoire* of the steel mill in the town of Hagondange, nestled just inside France's borders with Luxembourg and Germany, a dozen miles north of Metz and just inside the Maginot Line.

I long wondered: Why that move to a small industrial town in France? Why didn't my father move back to Vilna, the still-vibrant Jewish city within a city? Was he so concerned about finding work after college that he jumped at the first nearby opportunity? His work ethic and search for stability were evident when he took his young family from post-war New York City, with its vibrant Jewish life, to Cranston, a small, quiet city south of Providence, Rhode Island, to take a steady job with the local electric company – a job he kept for 20 years.

Only recently did I understand that my father's move westward at age 20, across the Rhine, was informed by what he saw as France's enlightened treatment of Jews, and the darkening clouds of antisemitism in Poland and Germany.

I know nothing about my mother's education or employment, just that she was a secretary for a time. I now realize that each parent kept – and later in life talked about – what meant most to them: my father, his high school diploma; my mother, her photos of friends.

By the mid-1930s my father was a successful young professional, fully established in France, while my mother, to judge from the dozens of snapshots she carried with her to America and the stories she told me as a child, was completely immersed in the social whirl of Jewish Vilna's high society. (Many photos bear dates and notes on the back in Russian, Polish, Hebrew, Yiddish, or French.)

My mother had a serious boyfriend, Volodia ("Volia"). In her photo album, there are 17 shots of Volia from 1936 to 1938, the year she married my father. When my mother and I would pore over her photo album together, I was only vaguely attentive to images of people I would never know, but I still remember how often she would pause wistfully to show me pictures of Volia. Rugged and handsome, with a shock of hair swept back, he appears in one photo from May 1937 linked arm-in-arm with my mother, as they look adoringly at each other (photo 4).

Volia seems to have been the opposite of my father: He was a sporty crew member, an avid clubman, and the life of the party. He was closer in age to my mother and shared her fun-loving spirit. Volia was the one who owned the box camera and wooden tripod, and his family's apartment was lavish, with paintings, ornately carved furniture, and a large wrought-iron balcony.

What happened? Why had Anna ("Niuta") thrown off Volia for that older bald man Isaac ("Izia") working in a French steel mill – someone who had been out of town for 16 years? I can never know for sure.

I do know that the Klauzner and Spokoiny families were among the intellectual and religious elite of Jewish Vilna. They were neighbors as well, and their children knew each other. My father's sister Rasha and my mother's brother Kolia had a long courtship and sometimes double-dated, as at the Lawyers' Ball, with Niuta and Volia. In fact, they were married on the same day as my parents in an April 1938 double wedding.

The wedding photo appears so suddenly in the album that it looks as if Volia has been swapped out of the picture for Izia at the last minute.

But why?

Was my mother's choice based on her sense of the disaster awaiting the Jews of Vilna? Perhaps she believed that my father would get her out of harm's way. Or was her decision more prosaic, reflecting the tough choices that any young woman might face as she selects her life mate? Did she feel that it was time to abandon that dashing socialite and settle down with a more serious man with an established position?

My mother had long known and admired – perhaps secretly loved – my father. I say this because of two photographs, one from 1930 and the other from 1937 (photos 5 and 6). The first, taken when he was 27 and just beginning his career at the Hagondange steel mill, and she was 21, shows my father, nattily dressed and commandingly serious, as the center of attention among a group of adoring young women. He knows he is admired, and he clearly likes it. My father's hand rests on the shoulder of his sister Rasha, who is kneeling next to her boyfriend and future husband, Kolia. As I read this picture, Izia is cozying up to Niuta, just behind and to his right. Her expression lies somewhere between dazzled and dazed. She knows something is going on, and another girl in the photo does too, as she looks directly into the camera's lens with a knowing smile.

The second photo, shot on June 10, 1937, is a coquettish closeup portrait of my mother; it is one of several that Volia took one day on the large balcony of his family's handsome apartment. (The sunlight on the balcony was ideal for his simple Polish box camera.) My mother is smiling both at the person taking the photo and the person to whom she gave the photo: my father, in faraway Hagondange. In an affectionate note on the back, she explains that the photo is a souvenir of long years of friendship, in memory of the many life lessons Izia has taught her through his stories. (This is the always-instructing father I knew as a child.) She finishes with an apology that the photo was taken from an angle that does not show her at her best.

Volia added affectionate notes to my mother on the back of several photographs of himself, including one taken on the very same day. He uses words like "dear little one," "angel," and "Niusiatse," a particularly sweet diminutive form of Niuta. The last photo from Volia, a forlorn studio headshot, is dated April 10, 1938, just two weeks before my parents' wedding.

The year 1937 was decisive. On August 10th, my mother took a ten-hour train ride from Vilna to Warsaw, to the French Consulate, to secure a 15-day visa to visit France, "on the occasion of the International Exhibition of 1937." The next day she went to the German and Belgian Consulates for transit visas. On August 14th she crossed the Polish border into Germany on the overnight train from Warsaw. Her destination was not the *Exposition Internationale*, though she paid the fee of 2,800 francs (about $50) to attend, but rather Metz, and a rendezvous with my father and his brother Misha (photo 7).

At first, I saw this visit as a bold act of courtship: Izia calling Niuta to France to propose marriage. But then why didn't he travel to Vilna to formally propose to her and meet with her formidable father?

I now believe that by the time of the Metz visit, the decision to marry my father had already been made by an agreement between my father and my grandfather. This was not a trip to advance their courtship, but rather a trip to introduce my mother to what would be her new home country, France. At the same time, it marked a decisive end to her romance with Volia.

There was likely a sense of urgency provoked by unfolding events. Józef Piłsudski, the father of modern Poland, had died in the spring of 1935. He believed that his country should be a "home of nations," and it was under his Second Polish Republic that the Jews of Vilna enjoyed their brief golden age.

With his death, acts of overt antisemitism became commonplace. Then, in the fall of 1936, my father's parents, his brother Israel, and sisters Genia and Sarah emigrated to Palestine. They were among tens of thousands of other European Jews who were then making the *Aliyah*, the "going up" to the Jewish holy city of Jerusalem, in response to the Zionist movement, which had begun slowly in the late 19th century. Between 1931 and 1936 the number of Jews in Palestine nearly doubled, to 370,000, which was more than a quarter of the population.

And most decisive, in 1937 my father paid a visit to his father's younger brother, who owned a pharmaceutical factory in Germany. He recounted that visit in the *Rhode Island Herald*, an English language Jewish weekly, in an article entitled "Remembrance…of Not So Long Ago" that he offered to mark Holocaust Remembrance Day, April 28-29, 1979.

On the newspaper stands I saw the most anti-Jewish paper, Der Stürmer. *On billboards I saw anti-Jewish slogans, like "Deutschland wake up, Judah drop dead." In Berlin I saw a huge Nazi parade and I heard anti-Jewish songs. I felt the satanic power of the Germans and it gave me the shivers.*

My uncle lived in agony. Torn between hope and despair, he was helpless. He wanted to escape but waited to sell his business.

My father concluded by saying that his uncle had "waited too long."

My mother may have felt that she had waited long enough for her dreamboat with the wavy hair. I recently discovered a revealing letter from her in a box of memorabilia squirreled away in the attic over our garage. She wrote it to me in May 1967, as I was about to finish my senior year at Bryn Mawr. In it, my mother offers heartfelt advice about my college boyfriend, about whom I was beginning to have serious doubts.

> *I know from my past how painful waiting, and hoping is.*
> *The only way to get over it – is to cut it out completely, only*
> *then you'll be able to forget. Well, do it, without hesita-*
> *tion.… He is a silly boy, not the man of your dreams.*

While talking about my life and my boyfriend Bob, my mother is also referencing her life and her boyfriend Volia – 30 years after their breakup. I have no doubt about that.

So, it seems likely that my father's decision to work in France was not an act of convenience but a strategic act of salvation prompted by his sense of impending doom, and my mother's decision was born of the mind and heart, when she finally decided to abandon her dashing, waffling sweetheart back in Vilna for that solid prospect whom she had long admired, and in some way loved.

My mother was back in Vilna on September 3rd, and, despite the trip, Volia had not gone away. Perhaps she led him to believe that she had gone to the International Exhibition in Paris.

I suspect so, since his last dated photo in her album, from the following April, is affectionately addressed to "Niusiatse." That was the month that my father came back to Vilna, to celebrate Passover and to marry my mother, in a double ring ceremony with Rasha and Kolia. This wedding took place on Sunday, April 24th, two days after Passover.

What was certainly my father's last trip back to Vilna was commemorated in a handsome studio photo showing the two new additions by marriage to the Spokoiny family, Izia and Rasha, behind the family's venerable patriarch, Rabbi Osher (photo 8).

I wonder: Did this turn of events come as a complete surprise to Volia?

My father then returned alone to his job in Hagondange, to await my mother, who for some reason didn't join her new husband until August. Her passport has a second visa issued by the French Consulate in Warsaw, this one dated August 4th and given for the express purpose of "contracting marriage." It was valid for one trip and eight days. On August 10th my mother's train crossed into Germany, and three days later, on Saturday, August 13th, she married my father in the town hall of Hagondange, at 11:30 A.M., before two witnesses: a Metz merchant named Othon Than and the mayor's secretary. April 24, 1938, was my parents' religious ceremony and the following August 13th their civil ceremony – in France, where they would make their home.

My mother moved into my father's house at 8 rue Roi Albert in Hagondange, which my father's brother Misha also called home. But I suspect that Misha knew, or was told, that it was now time to move on. Just weeks before the Vilna wedding, Misha joined the French Army.

Soon, my parents moved just a few hundred yards away into a handsome house with a garden at 55 rue des Alliés. Their honeymoon, though, would have to wait until February of 1939, when they made a grand tour of their adopted France, beginning in Paris and then on to Marseille, Monaco, and Nice. A photo captures the newlyweds in Nice, striding confidently down the Promenade des Anglais in smart outfits (photo 9).

Anna Spokoiny, a 28-year-old party girl, had married a 34-year-old grownup with a bright future and a nice home in France. This was the country of *liberté, égalité, fraternité* that, for the time being, was open and receptive to Jews. (Lorraine then had a relatively large number of Jews, and Metz several synagogues.) It was a land that, in Léon Blum, had a Jewish prime minister. In the process, my mother had been rescued from certain death had she stayed in Vilna.

In the honeymoon photo taken in Nice, the two look to be on top of the world. By then, they knew that my mother was pregnant with their first child, my brother Edmond. Eddy would be born in August 1939, just a month before Germany invaded Poland.

Extremely hard times lay just ahead. Did that newspaper tucked under my father's left arm give them hints of things to come? Could they have imagined in their wildest dreams – or in their darkest nightmares – that the most harrowing moments of their lives would unfold three years later in nearby Marseille?

SERPA PINTO

0   75   150   325   300

1 INCH = 75 MILES

TWO

FROM FRANCE TO THE SAFETY OF AMERICA

Five months after my parents' glamorous honeymoon on the French Riviera, my older brother, Edmond Sebastien, was born in the hospital of nearby Amnéville, on Friday, August 4, 1939 (photo 10; taken a few weeks before Eddy was born).

Within weeks, this young family would be torn apart by world events.

On August 23rd, Hitler and Stalin signed a non-aggression pact, including a secret protocol that put Vilna in the Soviet sphere of influence. (Stalin's troops entered the city on September 18th.) On September 1st the Nazis launched their blitzkrieg into Poland. Two days later, on September 3rd, France and the United Kingdom declared war on Germany, and World War II had begun.

Then, two days after that, my mother and brother were evacuated from Hagondange, directly inside the Maginot Line, to the Auvergne, a region in the center of France. A document drawn up on September 5th in the Hagondange mayor's office accompanied my mother and brother to Riom, a small city just north of Clermont-Ferrand, to be presented to the *Justice de Paix.* It explains the mandated transfer of the two on account of the "state of the infant's health" and "current events." A blurry photo, showing my mother and Eddy, is labeled "Riom, *Octobre* 1939." How did she manage the nine-hour ride in a packed train – including multiple connections – with a one-month-old baby, all by herself, while still recovering from childbirth?

My father stayed behind to put himself at the disposal of the mayor of Hagondange. No doubt his critical role as the head of the local steel mill's lab kept him out of the French Army.

When the War broke out, there were about 320,000 Jews in France, most of whom lived in Paris, although Lorraine had a relatively large number, in part owing to the recent influx of refugees from the East. And while Jews constituted less than 1% of the population of France, this was the highest proportion of any country in Western Europe. My parents were among the roughly one half of that 320,000 figure who were not French citizens, though my father, while still Polish, was set apart for having lived in France since 1923, and by his key position at a steel mill – an essential industry in wartime.

My father kept an important handwritten document with stamps and seals dated November 30, 1939, and signed by the director of the Hagondange steel mill, which is identified as a "war factory." It says that my father had been an engineer and chief of the steel mill's lab since April 1929 and that his attitude "*au point de vue national*" had never given any cause for reproach. It concludes *"en conséquence, je demande à l'Authorité Militaire de vouloir bien lui établir un sauf-conduit temporaire."* This is a request for my father to be granted "temporary safe conduct" by the French military authorities – no doubt, to visit his wife and four-month-old son in Riom.

A stack of snapshots captures a happy if brief reunion of the Klauzner family in Riom in January 1940. My parents and little Eddy are in the company of another family: Neil Kane, a pharmacist, and Anne, both Polish-born Jews, and their daughter Janet. My father had met the Kanes a decade earlier, when they lived in Thionville, just eight miles from Hagondange. The Kane family had since moved to Riom, a center of the French pharmaceutical industry, and, thanks to my father's friendship, took my mother and brother into their household. Neil Kane's clear affection for my brother in those photos suggests to me that he was Eddy's stand-in father when my parents had to be apart.

My father told me that when the Germans finally invaded France at lightning speed, he hopped on a retreating French army truck, and then asked the driver if they could stop at his house for a minute. He went in, looked around, and let the cat out. I am sure my father included the cat's escape in the story of his flight from Hagondange for my mother's sake, because she loved that cat, which she hugged in the photo taken just before Eddy was born. Years later, "Kitsy" was my mother's cherished cat in the United States.

My father never saw his Hagondange home again. That was June 6th, one day after the Germans launched *Fall Rot* ("Case Red") toward Paris, which they would enter, unopposed, on the 14th. By that time, millions of refugees had fled west and south. And just days later, Germany annexed Alsace and Lorraine.

My father soon reconnected with my mother and brother six hours to the west of Riom in La Rochelle, a port city on the Atlantic, where they found shelter in a beach shack without heat or indoor plumbing. They knew no one and were running low on savings. The only solution seemed to be to go to Paris, where my father could borrow money from relatives. Since there were no trains running, my father got an old bicycle, fastened his leather briefcase onto the handlebar, and headed for Paris, 300 miles away!

On the outskirts of the city, he learned that the Nazis had set up roadblocks and checkpoints, and that only vehicles with the proper documents could continue. (While the Nazis' antisemitic agenda was then clear, the roundup of Jews in Paris was still two years off.) My father started asking people for a ride. Finally, two men with a big truck put him and his bike beneath large sheets of leather they were transporting to a shoe factory. Their truck was stopped by the German police but not inspected. The problem, though, was that rats were hiding with my father under the tarp, nibbling away on the leather and crawling over him as they did.

I always believed that this encounter with rats was what drove my father later in life to take out the garbage seemingly by the hour, in small bags, to some location far from our house.

I try to imagine my father, then 37 years old, riding his bicycle from wherever that leather goods truck dropped him off, to the Marais, the now-fashionable district just northeast of Notre Dame Cathedral, where most of the Jews of Paris lived. There, I believe, he relied on the generosity of the Grinberg family, who were distant cousins.

It must have been eerily quiet, as tens of thousands of Parisians had left the city, and few non-military vehicles were allowed on the streets. In their place were bicycles and handcarts. Did my father take care to avoid the Place de la Concorde, knowing that the German High Command occupied the Hôtel de Crillon on its north flank? Perhaps he chose instead to take little side streets, so as not to be noticed. My father likely knew his way around, as Paris had been the first stop on his honeymoon, 17 months earlier.

I assume that my father chose La Rochelle to be as far away as possible from the German border. But the entire Atlantic Coast, for strategic reasons, was destined to become part of the Nazis' "occupied zone." So, like thousands of other Jews, the Klauzners soon made their way east and south, to the "free zone" governed by the Vichy regime.

But there was no escaping the grasp of the fascists, since the agenda of antisemitic laws and decrees was every bit as harsh in unoccupied Vichy France as in the Nazi-occupied north and west of the country. The Vichy regime's *Statut des Juifs* of October 3, 1940, was aimed at drastically reducing the role of the "Jewish race" in French society. Jews were now excluded from upper-level positions in the civil service and the army, as well as in professions that helped shape public opinion, such as radio, film, and theater. A quota system further limited their presence in the liberal professions, such as law and medicine. The lofty values of *liberté, égalité, fraternité* that I believe had brought my parents to France had been replaced by the new Vichy motto of *travail, famille, patrie*.

Late in life my father compiled a list of towns and cities in Vichy France where my family stopped in their travels, including Rodez, Toulouse, Montpellier, Nîmes, and Marseille. The list also included the internment camp at Gurs, in the foothills of the Pyrenees, near Pau, where my father's uncle – the one with the pharmaceutical factory in Germany – was confined with his wife, as expelled refugees from Nazi Germany (photo 11).

In his "Remembrance…of Not So Long Ago" article, my father wrote of his visit to his aunt and uncle in the *Camp de Gurs* in 1941.

> *Both were total wrecks. Uncle was repeating, "All was wrong, wrong…. All my life in Germany was a mistake." I*

*never saw them again. For a while we sent them packages
of food from the little we had ourselves. Shortly after, both
were deported to Poland and perished.*

What must have been going through my father's mind as he
passed food through the barbed wire to his desperate uncle and aunt:
that, but for fortune, their roles could have been reversed? He certainly
knew that had he stayed in Karlsruhe to finish his college degree and
taken a factory job nearby in the Baden region of Germany, he would,
by 1941, also be imprisoned with his family in Gurs.

My grandfather, Hayim, lived out his professional life in Vilna
as an accountant, emigrating to Israel in 1936 at age 64, with his wife
and three of his six grown children. Hayim's brother Gustave, with his
wife and their two young children, had emigrated to America in 1907,
when he was 32. Gustave had reached the rank of professor at St. Louis
University by 1941, when my father visited Gurs. Sadly, that brother
in Gurs, the youngest of the three, had chosen to make his career in
Germany. He and his wife were likely in their upper sixties when they
were deported from Gurs to Auschwitz and murdered.

According to family lore, it was always my mother who decided
when to move on, based on what she called her "premonitions" –
though my father had the papers needed to pass checkpoints in his
search for provisions. He would ride his bicycle to seek milk, bread,
and eggs, just as years later he and I would ride our bikes to do grocery
shopping in Cranston. It was the bicycle that made all this movement
possible.

Photograph 12 – dated June 1941 and taken near the village of
Ceilhes-et-Rocozels, about 60 miles northwest of Montpellier – shows
my family posed with two large skeletal bicycles, my father dapper in
a suit and beret, my mother chic in a suit and scarf. My father carried

Eddy in a basket attached to his handlebar, while his brother Misha took the back seat of the tandem bicycle.

Thirty years later, when Gary and I got married, my parents gave us bicycles as wedding presents. We asked for them because, I think, the bicycle has always represented my bond with my father. I also believed, through his war stories, that if all else fails, a bicycle is a guarantee of freedom. So, I have always thought of a bicycle as a necessity. After September 11, 2001 (which happened to be our 30th wedding anniversary), when the government sent out an advisory list for preparing an emergency escape kit, I made sure that our bikes were also ready, buying a new bicycle lock as well as a key to open the garage door manually if electrical power went out. I call this my "holocaust mentality."

As an *Ingénieur-Chimiste* with years of factory experience, my father was in high demand. From early January to mid-July 1941, he was employed in the mining operation in the village of Ceilhes-et-Ro-cozels. Then, from mid-July 1941 to mid-May 1942, he worked in the steel mill of the small industrial town of Decazeville, just over 100 miles northeast of Toulouse. I do not recall my father ever speaking about those two jobs, though the documents he left behind tell their own story – including his successful application in 1975 to the "*usine de Decazeville*" to claim his French social security benefits.

My father needed work, and the Vichy regime needed skilled workers to support its industrial output – which was put at the service of the Wehrmacht. And my parents must have known that. When the War broke out, the Hagondange steel mill was seized by the French government and became a "war factory," and its sister mill, in Deca-zeville, two years later, was certainly no less a "war factory" for the Vichy regime. My father's employment there began just weeks after

Hitler abrogated his non-aggression pact with Stalin and launched Operation Barbarossa, with the aim of conquering the Soviet Union – for which thousands of tanks were needed.

Working for the German war effort must have been a difficult moral bargain for my parents to strike, but it likely meant their survival.

During the two years between the outbreak of the War and the Nazis' push eastward in late June 1941, my father received "desperate letters" from Vilna. As he wrote in his account in the *Providence Journal*, "Nobody knew what to do."

Did my father learn that in those very weeks as he began work in Decazeville the Nazis were destroying Jewish Vilna? German forces entered the city on June 26th, four days after the launch of Operation Barbarossa. *Einsatzgruppe* (a mobile killing squad) B arrived a week later, and soon the killing of Jews began. The Nazis' eager Lithuanian collaborators were called, in Yiddish, *hapunes* ("snatchers") because they snatched their victims off the street. In the words of a contemporary Vilna diarist, "For the Germans 300 Jews are 300 enemies of humanity. For the Lithuanians 300 Jews are 300 pairs of shoes, trousers, and clothes."

Over that summer, the Nazis murdered 21,000 Jews, most shot and buried in mass graves at Ponary, a forested summer recreation area about seven miles south of the city. The Nazis chose this site because it was close to a railroad line and because a year earlier Soviet troops had dug huge round pits there for the storage of oil. By the end of 1941, the death toll had risen to 40,000, and by the end of the War, the number – more than 90% of the pre-War Jewish population of Vilna – had risen to over 70,000. This figure is close to the total number of Jewish Holocaust victims in all of France.

During my childhood in Cranston, a large photo in an elegant, old-fashioned frame, hung in my parents' bedroom (photo 8). I knew that this was my mother's family, and that the Nazis had murdered them all, except for my parents and an adolescent boy who had asked the Four Questions at their seder that year.

I do not recall that my mother conveyed this horrific information to me with great emotion. But I remember vividly her tears the day she heard from the Red Cross about the seder boy, who had survived the War because he was visiting a relative near the Russian border when the Nazis arrived and he ended up in a Russian orphanage. He declined contact with my mother because he was afraid of the Soviet authorities. My mother had finally lost him, too.

This formal and celebratory studio photograph commemorates both Passover 1938 and the double wedding between two families. The Spokoiny family, joined by two from the Klauzner family, appears carefully posed but also somewhat remote. To my eyes, the overall effect is royal. Yet this family portrait is at the same time utterly tragic; nine among the 12 will be dead in three years, along with two children not yet born.

We see my mother's parents seated in the front center, surrounded by their heirs. To the left is a family cluster of parents and two children, including my mother's sister Sonia (after whom we named our younger daughter), 39 years old, with her husband seated before her, and her two boys at their side. The couple standing next to the older child is my mother's sister Lisa (Alisa is the middle name of our older daughter) and her husband. Next to them is my father's sister Rasha and her husband, my mother's brother Kolia (after whom we named our older daughter, Nicole).

Kolia's story of heroism was much repeated in our household: He was a doctor in charge of a children's hospital, and when he refused to turn over the children for a roundup, the Nazis shot him on the spot. He could easily have saved himself, my father would say, since the Nazis needed doctors. Moreover, he had repeatedly turned down opportunities to emigrate to Palestine, because he felt an obligation to his hospital.

Rasha and Kolia had a daughter, Silvia, born in 1940. When the Nazis came to take Rasha from her apartment to the ghetto, she gave Silvia to a Christian neighbor. The child was sick, though, and died soon thereafter in a Jewish hospital. According to the list of family members my father compiled in the 1970s, all the other members of the Spokoiny clan died in 1941, presumably shot at the Ponary oil pits.

Misha and Grisha, two Vilna brothers who survived, had their own remarkable story, which seemed to me like a fairy tale, in part because of the singsong rhyming of the two heroes' names, and in part because their story sounded so unlikely. It seems that Misha and Grisha, my mother's cousins, made their living before the War by building sewer lines for the city. So, when the Nazis came for them, they went down into the sewers that they knew so well and sat out the War. A Christian friend and former employee would pass food down to them through a trap door. As it was so cramped in the pipes where they hid out, Misha and Grisha initially had difficulty walking upright when the Soviets liberated them. This is an odd story for sure, and my father loved to tell it.

Misha and Grisha, like Kolia, were in Papa's pantheon of war heroes, along with his uncle Gustave in St. Louis, who arranged for his entry visa to America.

Entry visas to the United States were increasingly difficult to come by, especially for Jewish refugees – due to America's deep-seated antisemitism. In the fall of 1940, President Roosevelt turned down a request from the Vichy regime to accept more than 6,500 mostly Jewish refugees that Hitler had just expelled from Germany.

By good luck, my father's American uncle, Gustave Klausner, had become friends with Harry Truman when Truman was elected senator in 1934; that same year, Uncle Gustave was elected president of the St. Louis Zionist Organization. That friendship resulted in the visa eight years later.

My father must have learned in early March 1942 that the U.S. government would grant an entry visa to the Klauzner family, including Uncle Misha, as he went to Rodez on March 19th to obtain his *Titre d'Identité et de Voyage*, into which an official at the U.S. Consulate in Marseille would stamp that visa.

Although he could not have known it, timing was critical, as Vichy France was gearing up to implement policies for the Final Solution to the "Jewish problem," drafted by the Nazi leadership at the Wannsee Conference in January. The first big roundup of Jews in Paris would take place in July, the same month that the yellow star became mandatory in the occupied zone.

On April 17th, the Klauzner family, with Misha, went to Marseille, more than 12 hours by train from Decazeville, to secure their entry visa to the United States from Leonard G. Bradford, American Vice Consul in the visa section of the American Consulate. I envision desperate crowds pushing and shoving to get in the door of the visa office, which was flooded with refugees fleeing the Nazi advance westward – as state-authorized translators press forward, prepared to take refugees' money to turn Polish, Lithuanian, and Russian documents into French, with just the right stamp. Whom could you trust?

The recent television series *Transatlantic* offers a sense of the desperation and chaos my family must have encountered in Marseille. It is a fictionalized account of the heroic, and sometimes illegal, efforts of Bradford's predecessor in the consulate's visa section, Hiram Bingham, Jr., in collaboration with the American journalist Varian Fry. Fry was working on behalf of the Emergency Rescue Committee of New York to get anti-Nazi (mostly Jewish) writers, artists, musicians, and intellectuals out of France. The urgency of their efforts, which unfolded from August 1940 to September 1941, was driven by a clause in the armistice agreement between Hitler and a defeated France that required the Vichy regime to arrest and surrender anyone the Nazis demanded. Fry and Bingham saved more than 2,000 refugees, including Marc Chagall and Hannah Arendt.

A photo taken on the way to Marseille, when the Klauzners met up with the Kane family in Nîmes, shows my parents gaunt and stressed (photo 13).

The black briefcase that my mother clutches in her right hand would have held the various documents they had assembled for their escape to America, including reissued birth certificates mailed in 1940 from Troki (for my father and uncle) and from Vilna (for my mother). That date tells me that the Klauzners had been planning their flight from Europe since soon after the War broke out.

How was the mail getting through to France – and to which address – from that far corner of Soviet-occupied Poland? And how did my parents find out which documents they needed, in what language, and with what official stamps and signatures? Because those birth certificates were written in Lithuanian, they had to be translated into French and stamped by an official translator – specifically, by a "Mme. N. Sabatier," who had set up shop next to the courthouse in Marseille.

I am certain that my parents never let that briefcase, which I recall from my childhood in Cranston, out of their sight.

Although that first trip had been a success, my father needed more documentation. On April 23rd, he made the full-day trip by train to Villefranche-de-Rouergue, to the office of the sub-prefecture of the Department of Aveyron, in which Decazeville is found, to secure his *visa de sortie* from France to the United States, via Marseille. The visa was valid for one month.

Were they all set?

Not at all. The worst possible news was yet to come: My father learned in late April of a recent Nazi order prohibiting any citizen of any country at war with Germany from leaving France. My parents were Polish citizens, and Poland had never formally surrendered to Germany.

At the same time, Vichy authorities ordered my parents to present themselves at the local police station in Decazeville. By then everyone feared that might mean arrest and confinement in the camp at Gurs, which my parents knew all too well.

As my father told it, an idea flashed through his mind: His brother Misha had received an official letter from the Polish government dated March 31, 1938, declaring him stripped of his citizenship for having joined the French Army. It occurred to him that Misha could claim that he was a stateless person, *"apatride,"* and thus avoid the prohibition and gain an exit visa from France.

My father thought of a clever way that he, too, could be "without a country." He made a copy of his brother's letter, typed his own name onto a small piece of paper and glued it over his brother's name, and brought the doctored document to a photographer to make a second, official-looking copy – likely in nearby Rodez, where on two occasions the Klauzners had arranged for fancy studio portraits of Eddy.

Fearing that the Vichy police might arrest him for his fishy-looking document when he returned to pick up its copy, my father asked his brother Misha to wait downstairs, below the photographer's studio, just in case. That way, he could warn my mother, and those two, with Eddy, could go into hiding.

With that photographic copy successfully in hand, my father returned to Marseille, this time alone. First, he needed its official translation into French, and for that, he chose from the Marseille phone book a Jewish lawyer named Levi, who assured him that he had done the right thing and arranged an authorized translation by his own daughter.

My father then took the forged document and its translation to the French police to request a second and final exit visa. Nervously, he presented his *Titre d'Identité et de Voyage* with its multiple official stamps and seals, along with his doctored photocopy, to the young woman in charge.

My father, who in my experience seemed incapable of lying, quickly broke down and confessed that the photocopy was a fraud.

The young woman said, "I will see what I can do for you."

After four days, on May 12th, my father returned to get the exit visa, once again fearing that the Vichy police might await him. But the same woman was there at the desk, and, with a slight smile but no words, she stamped his exit visa into his *Titre d'Identité et de Voyage*. My father said that she understood the situation perfectly well, and that she was a wonderful human being.

He wrote of this moment, "I confided in her; what else could I do? I saw with whom I am talking. I felt that she is an intelligent, fine woman. I do not know why. I felt if I do not tell the truth, I am lost."

I imagine my father looking even more anxious and dejected than in the photo from Nîmes – waiting for that young woman to reveal his family's fate. He always regretted not knowing her name and being able to thank her.

My father immediately telegrammed my mother to come to Marseille that night with Uncle Misha and Eddy.

They rushed to catch the midnight train. They were almost free, but there was yet another moment of fear.

At just under five feet, my mother was too small to carry her two-year-old onto the packed train, so she handed Eddy over to Uncle Misha as they boarded. As Misha's hands wrapped around Eddy, drawing him from my mother's arms, the lights went out. Screams, shoving, panic, as a stampede of desperate passengers pressed forward.

Suddenly my mother found herself alone.

Misha was gone, the baby was gone, and she was left in the darkness. The train was so crowded that she could not move and was unable to search for them.

She screamed, *"J'ai perdu mon bébé!"* ("I've lost my baby!")

As she told it, the people on the train lifted her up above their heads and "passed me hand to hand like a ball."

She went through car after car that way until she heard her child crying. She also heard what seemed like an echo through each car, *"La petite maman a trouvé son bébé!"* ("The little mother found her baby!")

After my mother, Eddy, and Misha reunited with my father in Marseille, the very next day, May 13th, the four boarded a ship for Morocco.

Afraid that the Germans might seize and search the ship, my father threw the falsified document into the sea.

But evidence of my father's scheme survives (photo 14). When he received his identity card in Rodez on March 19th, the official in charge entered "Polish" on the nationality line. But by the time Papa and his little family sailed out of the port of Marseille, "Polish" had been overstruck in red ink and replaced with "stateless," with the note that Isaac Klauzner had been stripped of his Polish citizenship on March 31, 1938 – which was, of course, the same date that Uncle Misha had been stripped of his Polish citizenship.

No doubt that "fine woman" behind the desk at the French police station in Marseille wrote those words.

There are no photos of Casablanca, where the Klauzner family stayed for nearly three weeks. Only a booklet of monochrome post-cards scribbled over in green crayon, no doubt by Eddy. Four of the 20 postcards in the booklet had been mailed, and a fifth, showing the Boulevard de la Gare, begins, in my mother's handwriting, *"6 Juin 1942 / Cher Monsieur / Au moment…."* I like to believe that on the day before their departure from Casablanca, when my family's fate was finally secure, my mother was sending word that the Klauzners were about to sail for America.

I also like to believe that the world my family inhabited for those weeks was a bit like Rick's American Bar in the film *Casablanca*, which came out that same year, 1942. Though with the difference that, unlike the desperate refugees in Rick's bar, my parents knew they had the right papers to get to America.

On June 7th, my family left Casablanca for New York City with 800 other passengers on board the Portuguese cruise ship the S.S. *Serpa Pinto*. In a dozen crossings, that ship bore more than 7,000 mostly Jewish war refugees across the Atlantic, via Lisbon and Casablanca, to destinations in Central and North America. If the Klauzners had taken the *Serpa Pinto* in September, as the Kane family did, the destination would have been Baltimore, where I now live.

The Klauzners arrived in New York City on June 25th. The sight of the Statue of Liberty must have profoundly impressed my mother, who had me memorize the famous poem by Emma Lazarus, "The New Colossus," which concludes with the words, "I lift my lamp beside the golden door!"

THREE

IMMIGRANTS ON COMMUNITY DRIVE

The headline in *The New York Times* on Thursday, June 25th, the day my family arrived at Ellis Island, read "Russian Marines Land in Crimea in Surprise Move to Aid Sevastopol." Further down, the front page notes that President Roosevelt and Prime Minister Churchill would address a joint session of Congress on their offensive strategy for the War.

But my parents must have simply been feeling relief: relief that they were finally on terra firma after 19 days at sea, and relief that they had at last reached a safe place.

On the ship's arrival manifest, under "ethnicity/nationality," the Klauzners are categorized by the word "Hebrew," which is found nowhere else among the many official documents that my parents brought with them in their black briefcase. My father is listed as "chemist," his brother as "mechanic." They have a nest egg of $200 and their official sponsor is listed as Gustave Klausner of St. Louis.

Gustave Klausner was born in Vilna in 1875, emigrated to the United States with his wife Anna, son Eli, and daughter Rebecca in 1907, and went to work as a clerk in the garment industry in St. Louis. Three years later, at age 35, he entered St. Louis University as a part-time student. Gifted and determined, Gustave went on to earn his Ph.D. and teach at the university for 35 years, eventually receiving an endowed professorship at the School of Commerce and Finance. On his retirement, the university's president described "Professor Gus" as "a superb teacher, an energetic civic and religious leader, and, above all else, a gentleman of unimpeachable integrity and genuine moral character."

My father had likely met his uncle Gustave at least once, during the latter's visit to Vilna in the early 1930s, when he posed for a photo with my grandfather.

As one of the pioneer American Zionists, Uncle Gustave worked to rehabilitate land in Palestine for a Jewish state; eventually, supporters planted 10,000 trees in a section of the Israel national forest named in his honor. In 1934, Uncle Gustave was elected president of the St. Louis Zionist Organization and later, vice-chairman of the Jewish National Fund.

No one was there to meet the Klauzners on that momentous day. Instead, like thousands of other Jewish war refugees, the four left Ellis Island and found temporary lodging at the Hebrew Immigrant Aid Society (HIAS) in Lower Manhattan, near New York University. With all my father's formidable language training, I wonder: Could he read or speak English when they arrived in America? I assume that he had been studying on his own for months before leaving Marseille. And certainly, most of the displaced Jews aided by the HIAS spoke Yiddish.

The Klauzner family, plus Misha, travelled by train to St. Louis in July, and for a few weeks lived with Gustave and his wife in their small garden apartment just north of Forest Park. I am sure that Gustave and Anna provided everything my family needed, but it must have been cramped, and with neither my father nor Misha yet working – and War rationing in effect – mealtime must have been a challenge, and noisy. Yiddish, Russian, or English? I would guess that my father insisted on practicing English at the dinner table.

Uncle Gustave was a family hero; a large photo of him in a handsome acrylic frame sat for decades on our upright piano, a place of honor, where we looked up to him daily. It was Uncle Gustave who had made it possible for us to live in America, and who continued to show support and affection. For my birthday each year he sent me a gift, usually a beautiful sweater, wrapped in a fancy box.

I was surprised to discover a photo of my father's draft registration card on Ancestry.com, as he had never mentioned that he might have been drafted into the U.S. Army. It was issued just weeks after the Klauzners disembarked in New York. And although America had been at war with Germany and Japan for six months, and things were looking grim in both Europe and the Pacific, I would not have guessed that a Polish refugee with limited English would so quickly have been drawn into the war effort. At age 39, my father was three years beyond the current upper limit for induction.

Misha, who had served in the French Army, chose to enlist in the U.S. Army the following March, and in July 1943 became a naturalized American citizen. (He had stayed on with Gustave and Anna in the interim.) Misha took the fast track, thanks to the Second War

Powers Act of 1942, which lifted some of the naturalization require-
ments for non-citizen servicemembers related to age, race, residence,
and education.

The third and fourth addresses (after the HIAS) on my father's
draft registration card are both from 1943: One, dated April 12th, is in
Spokane, Washington, and the other, dated July 23rd, is in the Bronx.
Spokane was a rapidly growing industrial hub supporting the war
effort, and my father often spoke of working there "for a year" – from
the summer of 1942 to the summer of 1943.

When I was born, on October 24, 1945, in Manhattan, our
family lived in the Sunnyside neighborhood of Queens. This address
fit well with my name, Elana, the Hebrew poetic word for "tree." I
believed (and Mommie reinforced my belief) that I was a tree planted
in the new world of freedom. In Sunnyside. And that embedded in my
middle name, Joyce, was the French word for joy, as in *élan de joie*, a
"burst of joy." And that the coupling of my birth with the first United
Nations Day, when the U.N. Charter was officially adopted, was nothing short of miraculous, as I embodied the hope for global unity after
the devastation of World War II. Surely, I was destined for a blessed
life (photo 15).

Papa was then employed in a chemical factory, but I don't recall
that he ever spoke about it. What counted were his studies. Around
the time I was born, he resumed his advanced schooling, which he had
abandoned in 1928, at New York University. At what now seems like
breakneck speed, Papa graduated with a master's degree in chemistry
in 1947, at age 44.

He then took the job of chief chemist at the Narragansett Electric Company in Providence, Rhode Island, arriving in early 1948.

According to family lore, part of the reason we left New York was that Misha's factory boss fired him for refusing to work on Shabbat, which Papa recognized as antisemitism in the most Jewish of American cities. Though there was no escaping it. At the electric company, Papa's nickname was "Ike," which some among his co-workers transformed into "Ike the Kike."

Oddly, despite all that Papa and Misha (who was six years younger) had gone through before and during the War, I never sensed great affection between them. Nor that Papa was proud of him, as he was proud of his brother Israel, the historian and writer who had emigrated to Palestine in 1936. Misha, who had dropped out of high school, was quiet, and like his wife, who typically spoke for the family, deeply religious. As I follow the trail of my parents' turbulent lives from their rendezvous in Metz in the summer of 1937 to their arrival with Eddy in St. Louis in the summer of 1942, it seems to me that Misha was always "tagging along." And that Papa was always taking care of him, including assembling the necessary papers for his passage to America.

I suspect that Uncle Misha was not too bright, and that Papa, the oldest son, felt responsible for him – just as, in the late 1920s, he had felt responsible for the medical school expenses of his younger sister Sarah. Where was Papa's father in all of this? He had emigrated to Palestine in the fall of 1936 and died in Jerusalem in June 1938, just two months after my parents' Passover wedding in Vilna – at age 66.

Did Papa resent Uncle Misha for the burden he represented? Did he ever feel that Israel, his younger brother who succeeded so spectacularly and publicly in Israel, had gotten the breaks denied to him? I can never know for certain, but I never sensed either of two telltale emotions in Papa: jealousy or resentment.

As for me, I felt little emotional connection to Misha's family, though I loved our springtime visits to their apartment in New York City, and the marvelous sponge cake that Misha's wife, Shulamith, would bake for us.

Once in Rhode Island, we Klauzners settled into a second-floor apartment in a large house with a wide porch at 91 Wheeler Avenue in Cranston, a small city just south of Providence. That Wheeler Avenue apartment, where we would stay for the next five years, was our family's first real home since Hagondange and the outbreak of World War II. It was positively cozy, with its warm hardwood floors and elegant colonettes.

I think of Eddy during the first decade of his life, fleeing from Hagondange to Riom to La Rochelle, then to the French free zone, and the little mining town of Ceilhes-et-Rocozels and the scruffy steel mill town of Decazeville. And then on to America by way of Casablanca. At the age of three, he moved from New York City to St. Louis, and then on to Spokane. As I was born and Papa attended NYU, Eddy was moved from the Bronx to Queens.

How did school go for him in those years? Eddy's first language was French, and our parents were themselves just learning English. He turned out to be a brilliant student, entering Harvard at 17, but that first decade of his life must have been difficult. For my part, my first memories of our Wheeler Avenue apartment and Norwood Avenue Elementary School (in fact, a large frame house) are glowing.

The extraordinary year of 1948 was capped off in November by my parents getting their naturalization papers and officially changing their name to Klausner, to match the version of the name shared by relatives in both Israel and the United States.

In 1953, our little family – Papa, Mommie, Eddy, and me, Kukla ("Doll" in Russian) – moved into our own house with our own backyard on the most American of American streets (photo 16). Ours was a small Cape Cod at 33 Community Drive. At 1,200 square feet, with three bedrooms and one bath, it was like all the other houses on our block in the Edgewood neighborhood, laid out in 1946 to accommodate Cranston's post-war population boom.

This was my Jewish immigrant version of the home in my favorite TV show, *I Remember Mama*, about a Norwegian immigrant family in San Francisco. I believed that our home, like theirs, would be a warm and loving retreat for a family new to America, a family with heavy accents, odd customs, and little money. And so it turned out to be, and it will always remain my version of what a growing-up home is all about. Because it was there that, between the ages of 8 and 18, I became me.

This is where my parents would remain for the next 40 years; and where Eddy and I, with our spouses, would return for birthdays and Passover. In that same kitchen with that same Formica table. This is the place where the Klausners gradually transformed themselves from immigrants into Americans.

Papa, with Eddy's help, seemed constantly to be working on the house's exterior and in the yard. He was clearly proud and protective of his new home, after 15 years on the move. Papa would sometimes burn old paint off the wood with a scary electric device that looked like a flat iron. He would then freshen up the bricks with red paint. A scrawny but fragrant lilac tree stood on the side of our small back yard, and rose bushes flanked the front steps, which led directly into the living room. I do not recall that my parents were particularly friendly with others on the block, whom we believed to be mostly Catholic. Still, Papa was sensitive to what they thought of him, and so he and Eddy kept the grass cut and the hedge that separated us from the O'Learys neatly trimmed.

A photo of Mommie and me taken shortly after we moved in shows our small living room decorated pretty much as I recall it decades later. The fireplace was never used, and a beige carpet covered the hardwood floor. The bookcase was filled with Hebrew books, the side tables with stacks of popular magazines – *LIFE*, *Reader's Digest*, *TIME* – and newspapers in English, Yiddish, and French. Papa's NYU diploma hung in the short hall connecting our kitchen to the living room. Mid-century lamps brightened the display of various exotic artifacts from Israel, a Russian samovar, and two Chinese vases brought by the mysterious "Mr. Friend." He, a Polish Jew, had escaped the Nazis by way of Shanghai, and his one visit, which I noted in my diary at age eight, was extremely exciting, especially as he brought me a tiny gold ring. There was a sofa and two large chairs upholstered in a green scratchy wool, which were covered in the summer with botanical slip covers. Much later, these were replaced by a leather set, bought in Denmark and shipped home. This surprised and impressed me, given how careful Papa was with money, after years of just scraping by.

The first floor also included a small kitchen, an enclosed but unheated back porch, my parents' bedroom, our one bathroom (tiled in 1940s pink and black), and our tiny den, with upright piano and television. A stairwell with a glass block window led up to two bedrooms beneath sloping eaves. My bedroom, facing the back yard, had been newly "finished," so I had low, built-in drawers, as well as a chest and desk. My closet was a sloped add-on in the hall. Its interior, just like my bedroom, was wallpapered in a gorgeous purple floral pattern, which matched my comforter. These were produced by the venerable Schumacher Company, which I realized only as an adult. Like the Danish leather furniture, this extravagance surprised me.

Eddy's room was home to a jumbo fan on a stand, which pulled in a great breeze on sweltering summer nights from his set of windows across the hall. A big unfinished closet in the hall was meant to become a second bathroom, but it never did. Instead, it held lots of clothes, as did our large, dry, unfinished basement, with clotheslines for the laundry and storage for all kinds of things, including an old zither, a console radio, rows of garment bags, a rack of ironed shirts near the ironing board, canned goods, and tools. Our garage was barely large enough to hold a car, and since Papa usually nudged the back wall when he parked, it bowed out.

Just as the second bathroom was never added, the back porch was never winterized. So, I suppose that 33 Community Drive was, for Mommie and Papa, good enough the day they walked in. Papa was cautious with money, and though my mother's childhood apartment had been fancier, she never complained.

My school friends, none of whom were children of immigrants, lived in other, non-working-class neighborhoods, in bigger, more elaborate houses. But I never felt embarrassed when my friends came over, even when they giggled about our garage's bowed-out back wall. For me, social class was defined not by money but rather by education.

Our kitchen – or rather, what happened in our kitchen – also set my family apart from my friends' families. This tiny room was painted a pale apple green, above speckled beige tiles with black trim. Over time, it acquired a dull, greasy patina that Papa's janitor friend from work would wash away. Just to the left as you entered from the hall was our stove, whose oven stored our writing supplies: pencil jars, rulers, rubber bands, pads of paper, and notebooks. This mystified my friends, especially since I had no explanation. Though perhaps this was simply old-world caution: Gary's thesis advisor at Princeton, who was the same age as Papa and with his wife had also fled Hitler, kept books in his oven.

Because I could never bake brownies, I resigned myself to making Jell-O and chocolate pudding, "pitching" them, as I worked, to the housewives of my imagined television audience. (My sales pitch always began, "Ladies, are you out of ideas for a dessert that your whole family will love? Then try…."). Mommie turned to a special countertop appliance for roasting chicken and a domed stove-top apparatus for baking potatoes. One electrical outlet under the wall clock featured a precarious multi-plug tangle of wires and extension cords, which was dangerous, and odd for an employee of the electric company.

Mommie's *batterie de cuisine* was so limited and old-world that I always assumed it came over with her on the boat. She had told me that going to America was "like going to another planet." There was her two-handled egg pan, which I still have, with its missing wooden handle, its multiple dents, and its soft, hazy silver patina from decades of use. And her potato masher, which was missing a rivet and so had to be carefully aligned with her small French saucepan, whose wooden handle was loose and could easily cause a disastrous tip-over. A few years ago, while staying in a friend's Paris apartment, I was startled to discover an identical saucepan with a loose wooden handle. This convinced me that all three – the egg pan, the potato masher, and the saucepan – had come down the ramp of the S.S. *Serpa Pinto* in my parents' suitcase.

Breakfast was scant, as Papa left for work at 5:30 A.M., reappearing at about 6:30 P.M. from his second job, teaching Hebrew. He did, however, squeeze fresh orange juice every morning. Once, when I was about four, I tried to throw away some pulpy juice. Papa blew his top – not, I think, because of his wasted effort, but because after years of hardship he could not stand the thought of wasting food. As he could not stand the thought of wasting time.

Mommie slept in, as she liked to stay up late to watch Jack Paar or read her women's magazines (one of her few luxuries), including *McCall's*, out of which I cut all the Betsy McCall paper dolls, as well as every version of Campbell Soup Kids, to be pasted into a scrapbook that I still have. Mommie was annoyed to find out that I had reported to my kindergarten teacher that she did not make my breakfast. She likely did, but then rushed right back to bed, "making" my ponytail from a reclining position. In high school I would eat half my lunch in place of breakfast on my way to school.

Often Eddy and I carried our dinner to the den, moving the piano bench to use as a table, watching TV – and jumping up at each ad for him to stand at the piano and me to sing into our goose-necked lamp. Papa had made four blocks of wood with countersunk circles to raise the piano bench for me, and I would skate around the room on two of them in time to Eddy's music. After years of use, their bottoms had become smooth and slippery.

Our menu differed from those of my friends as well. It was not that we kept kosher, although we never drank milk until after dinner, with dessert, and we never had bacon at home, frying up kosher baloney instead. (Though Mommie would, as a treat at the Newport Creamery, order a BLT on toast and ask them to skip the lettuce and tomato; the word "hold" was not in her idiomatic range.) We ate sardines and smoked white fish, artichokes, and cold beet soup.

Peanut butter on crackers was only to take to the beach, Mommie openly disdaining it as a "common" lunch choice.

Dinner was a full-blown home-cooked special, with a first course, meat and potatoes and salad, and dessert. A classic Klausner meal would begin with half a grapefruit with sugar, followed by a three-cornered pot roast seared and simmered with canned mushrooms for four hours, hand-made mashed potatoes with lots of butter, a salad of iceberg lettuce with a sweet dressing of lemon juice, sugar, salt, and cooking oil – and finally, my chocolate pudding. Another favorite dish was a simple rice soup, made with rice, milk, and sugar. We always had dark pumpernickel bread, and wonderful cinnamon sticks and cheese Danishes ("cheesies") from Korb's Bakery. My parents drank the old European standby, Nescafé instant coffee, with evaporated milk and sugar. Our stash of evaporated milk cans was lined up on a basement shelf, alongside the assorted chemicals brought home from "the plant" for Eddy's science experiments. I would go down and fetch some cans, making Mommie guess how many I had chosen to carry up.

Some of my parents' personal habits struck me as strange. For example, there was Mommie's single daily Viceroy cigarette, smoked in the bathroom, and Papa's old-world way of eating bread by tugging pieces out of the loaf with the fingers of his right hand. His fingers were short and wide, like hammers, perfect for his piano style, which was banging. That is my style as well, but I have learned to tame it.

Much like we Klausners had our own concocted version of keeping kosher, we had a mélange of religious observances and beliefs – all centered on Temple Beth Israel. Papa took the lead, as he faithfully went to temple every Saturday morning, and often on Friday evening as well. On weekdays he would sometimes wrap himself with two small leather prayer boxes with straps, known as *tefillin* (one on his arm and one on his forehead), and pray at home. Papa was often called by the rabbi to the *bimah*, or central platform, to chant directly from the Torah scroll. Mommie accompanied him only on the high holidays or on special occasions. While Eddy was a dutiful bar mitzvah boy, at that time it was not considered necessary for girls to follow suit with a bat mitzvah. I was confirmed, which entailed classes at the synagogue, solo prayer singing at Friday night service, and a special ceremony, which I happily performed.

I enjoyed the foreign language of Hebrew and treated going to Beth Israel as a social occasion: an opportunity to meet and flirt with Jewish boys from other schools in the area. These boys taught me bowling, driving, and a bit of tennis, and I went to many more proms than I might otherwise have. Thus, I was eager to attend synagogue, as it seemed a happy place. Though Papa would send me out of the sanctuary during the recitation of the Mourner's Kaddish, as some among the congregants would weep, and perhaps he would as well.

Papa had taught me the Old Testament stories as a young child and provided me with rational explanations for the advent and triumph of Christianity, as well as the history of antisemitism. In high school, a Catholic classmate once told me that as a Jew I would burn in hell for having killed Christ. It stuck with me, and I latched onto any notion that would dispel this stigma. I became particularly taken with the idea that, as one of Christ's best friends, Judas took on the duty of betraying Christ to help him fulfill his mission. Otherwise, I always felt an affinity with Catholic kids, as they prayed in Latin and had the burden of guilt.

I no longer attend services or fast on Yom Kippur. Chanukah is a family obligation. But Passover is still a major holiday in our household, which I cherish. I am proud that our daughter Sonia believes in God, despite Gary's professed atheism and my waffling on the issue, but I am dismayed that Nicole has no desire for her children to know the Bible, even though they know every other mythology on earth. I will try to take care of that facet of their education!

Going out was always a *thing* because we did not own a car until I was 11. This meant a lot of walking, taking buses, and asking for rides. Once, at a bus stop, under pouring rain, Papa stuck out his thumb and someone picked our wet selves up to go downtown. Worse was grocery shopping, which Mommie did not do, save for making a list. Papa and I would set out with either a big old baby carriage, a sled, or our bicycles, and the distance seemed painfully long.

On one memorable occasion, Papa and I were riding our bikes home from the store through Roger Williams Park. We both had paper bags of food. (I was always embarrassed at Papa's assumption that he could help himself to a few extra paper bags from the cashier's pile.) That day Papa's overflowing bag broke open, scattering tomatoes all over the street. We both scrambled to gather them up. My friend Fredda recalls my saying in high school that "this was one of the closest moments I ever had with my father."

This bonding episode clearly meant much to me, since I made it the subject of an essay for my advanced composition class in the spring of my senior year. The essay focused on our immigrants' moment of "them versus us." I was both embarrassed and defensive for Papa. I knew that we stood out as odd in our suburban neighborhood, where everyone else went shopping for groceries in their car. I was terrified that the tomatoes would be squashed and that all traffic in Roger Williams Park would come to a standstill. And I desperately wished that we could afford a car.

I wrote in my essay that "Cars stopped; a woman flung open her car door and screamed words I had never heard before; a teenage girl licking an ice cream cone walked by and laughted hysterically. I looked at her accusingly."

My father said nothing, nor did I, but I knew that we were feeling the same emotions, and that brought us closer.

My scrapbook has a section called "My Life in Pictures," where I wrote, "It all really began when…" near photos of our first car, a 1953 Buick Roadmaster, which Papa bought used in 1957, not long after the tomato debacle. Eddy, who took driver's training, is behind the wheel, as we are about to head out on a bona fide road trip to New Hampshire. Somehow Papa eventually learned to drive, though poorly, as he could not refrain from nosing into traffic at every intersection. Mommie never even tried to learn to drive. But having a car meant that we were at last in the mainstream of motorized American life.

Linguistic Vilna lived on in our Cranston home, as I heard Russian, French, Hebrew, Yiddish, and occasionally even German. Or so I believed, since to my childhood ears it was all melded into what I considered gibberish. In this, I knew that I differed from my friends, even my Jewish friends.

First off, I heard mostly Russian at home, and yet I was spoken to by my parents in their newly acquired version of English. My brother had the added layer of his childhood French to deal with.

We never knew what our parents were talking about. Or rather, shouting about, as they were often agitated and loud. This shouting bewildered and frightened me, since I assumed that they were angry and discussing my brother and me. I found what I took as confirmation in one turn of phrase that was their translation from the French "*demander pardon*." Eddy and I were perpetually "begging pardon" for our misdeeds.

What were our sins? Mostly academic: less than perfect grades. Though not practicing the piano was also a grave issue. And just "hanging around" was unforgivable. I would have my legs slung over the big armchair, and Papa would ask, "Are you going to just sit around and stink?" (Better to read a book.) "Begging pardon" in the Klausner household was the formal act on the part of Eddy or me of begging forgiveness from Papa for a specific misdeed. This was usually followed by reconciliation, namely, sitting in Papa's lap – which was especially awkward once Eddy had grown up.

Eddy would play the most wonderful modern jazz on the piano, by ear, which Papa would denounce as "junk." Our parents considered a few of our friends to be "common," and so maybe they, too, were subjects of the late-night shouting matches.

I spent countless hours guessing what their words might mean and creating scenarios with dialogues. Frustrating though that was, making associations within and between languages became one of my strongest skills. My diary entry on the first of the year, 1959, when I was 13, declares, "Guess what! I know some words in Russian. Boy – I used to think the word 'liver' was 'cookie'!" The two, in fact, differ in Russian by just two letters – *pechen* versus *pechen'ye* – so I was dead wrong but on the right track.

My parents' English, while understandable, came with a heavy old-world accent as well as many odd turns of phrase, which I eventually understood to be "immigrant English." For instance, my mother would "make me a ponytail," while Fredda's mother would "fix her hair." (I still say "cut me some cake," to the amusement of my husband.)

In an article in the *Providence Journal* in 1986, my father described the dark bread of his youth: "You had to have a stomach from iron to digest it because it was so grainy."

I carry a flavor of that immigrant-English phraseology to this day and was not flattered when my dissertation advisor told me that I wrote better in French than in English.

I also heard my parents speak and sing in Yiddish with their small band of local friends – people with very thick accents. I would sit quietly, bored, but diverted at one house by a clever German Shepherd who could catch and crack walnuts with his teeth, and at another by the secrets (medicine bottles) hidden within a bathroom medicine cabinet.

Then there were the local Yiddish actors, Israel and Esther Barenboim, whose son had been taken to the internment camp at Drancy, north of Paris, and then shipped to Auschwitz, where he was murdered. Papa accompanied them as they practiced songs for meetings of the Farband Association, which was devoted to preserving and developing Yiddish culture. I always found their quavering voices revoltingly sentimental.

Yiddish seemed old and embarrassing, just like the Yiddish word "schmaltz," which means chicken fat. I would want to run out when the dramatic singing and banging on the piano began, just as I wanted to escape from our house every time it had the pungent smell of kasha (buckwheat groats), at least as Mommie prepared it. I admit, though, that I still use the Yiddish phrase "It's a *meshuggeneh velt*" – "crazy mixed-up world."

I came to believe in the superiority of Hebrew as the authentic ancient, specifically Jewish, language, in part because every week we would receive a wispy, pale blue airmail letter from relatives in sunny Israel, written in densely scrawled Hebrew. I would dutifully sign my name in Hebrew when my parents wrote back, just as I signed my daily diary in Hebrew. I was amazed at how proficient Papa was in Hebrew, and how capable he was in reading the Torah at our temple, as well as preparing scores of boys facing their Haftorah reading for their bar mitzvah. While in his eighties, Papa was still active in our local Jewish community in efforts to create Hebrew-speaking study groups and in reviving Yiddish.

Papa cleverly got me to take Hebrew lessons from him by offering to include my best friend Fredda in the class. We both have positive memories of these weekly lessons at our kitchen table. My group classes, unlike my one-on-one lessons for piano, math, and science, were never tense. Fredda, later a student at the Rhode Island School of Design, gave me a small sketchbook with a drawing of our childhood Hebrew lessons, where we both appear to be giggling.

We two had weekly French lessons with Papa as well, joined by our friends Dayle and Karen. Here I was highly motivated, aware even in elementary school that I wanted to speak French fluently and travel to France one day. Languages were simply an integral part of my everyday life.

I saw my parents' arsenal of linguistic skills put to effective use every spring, when our family enjoyed its annual trip to New York City by train during my school break. Mommie and I, in our finest outfits, would go to art museums, to our favorite lunch spots, and to the big department stores to shop, while Papa made it a point to take me to the gorgeous Librairie Française at Rockefeller Center to select a new French book.

During these magical holidays, we would also wait in line for what seemed like hours to get into Radio City Music Hall. When I was 11, I described in my diary the full Radio City experience, including the new movie *Funny Face*, the Rockettes with their "precision kicking," and the candelabras, thick rugs, and mirrors, as well as the ornate downstairs bathroom. For my parents, though, the spring trip offered an equally magical opportunity to catch up with their European friends – in whatever language was appropriate.

In Manhattan, my parents spoke English with my uncle Misha, as his wife was American. But with their Jewish friends from France whom they met on the boat, they spoke French, which I really loved, especially as that couple had a handsome son one year older than me named Robert, who played the violin. In the Bronx, my parents spoke Yiddish with their friends Helen and Jacob, whose daughters were named Rozzie and Beverly.

When I was five, we went to Beverly's wedding in a grand hotel. It was thrilling. I wore a red and white checked organdy pinafore dress with a white organdy coat, as well as a homemade blue satin gown for the actual wedding. All of us children ran up and down the grand staircase and got ice from machines to our heart's content, as a cacophony of Yiddish and Russian buzzed in the distance. We felt this burst of energy to run free because, for once, we could. Typically, we would be stuck for hours with our parents and their Bronx friends in their kitchen, as they jabbered away in a language we could not decipher.

With friends in Brooklyn, my parents spoke English, and I marveled at kids calling up from the street to get their friends to come out to play. It was there that I developed the habit of "calling for" my two best friends in Cranston. I would stand outside and twice call out in a sing-song way "Hey Fre-dda-a!" or "Hey Day-Day!" (for Dayle).

It was inevitable that after years of Russian language studies I would eventually figure out what my parents were shouting about in the middle of the night. And I was shocked. Now imagine the scene: My (then boyfriend) Gary and I have come up from Princeton for a visit, and we are sleeping on the rollout in the den – which is just opposite the door to my parents' bedroom. It is 4:00 A.M. and dead quiet on Community Drive. Suddenly, we are jolted awake.

Mommie is shouting in Russian, "Kiss my ass!"

Papa is shouting back, simultaneously and at the same elevated pitch, "Burn in hell!" Then one or the other (perhaps both) retorts with the ultimate insult, "Mop the floor with your mother's ass!"

This astounded me, especially given how proper my parents always were in English and how little tolerance Papa had for others cursing around him. Once in high school, after an especially difficult piano lesson, I shouted, "Damn Bach!" Papa, the ever-so-serious student of the Torah, exploded.

And I am sure the night Gary came to visit, I was the subject of their shouting match, for bringing that blond non-Jew home.

BRYN MAWR COLLEGE

0   50   100   150   300

CRANSTON, RI   BRYN MAWR, PA

1/2" = 50 MILES

FOUR

BRYN MAWR AND "NOBLENESS TO SOCIAL AIMS"

Even as a child I knew that Papa's dream for me – as well as for Eddy – was to be intellectually engaged at the highest level of education. "You can lose everything, but no one can take away your education," he would often say.

Our family values did not include social climbing or making money. We were impressed by a person's education and artistic achievement. In my diary I gushed over the "genius" Charles van Doren and never suspected that the quiz show *Twenty-One* was rigged.

By the age of 12, I had become an intellectual snob.

Papa's expectations and my hard work would pay off in ways neither of us could have imagined. In truth, I always liked being a student and even the challenge of taking tests. I assume I inherited that from Papa. In sixth grade I wrote to my diary, "I can't believe that I was one of the few that got straight A's two terms.… Later, I was almost crying because everybody said I got good marks because I'm his pet. Mr. Curran said, 'They are jealous.'"

Now I wonder if I had bragged by announcing my grades. Or if I secretly feared that I did not deserve them. But I have always worked hard to please my favorite teachers, including Mr. Curran, whom, I now suspect, I must have seen as other versions of Papa. Even today, I am thrilled when my piano teacher says, "You're such a good student. You practice whatever I ask you to work on."

My years at Park View Junior High launched my commitment to French and introduced me to the art of diagramming sentences, which I loved. At Cranston High East I had the opportunity to start Russian. This offering directly followed the Soviet launch of Sputnik under Khrushchev, a wakeup call for the United States during the Cold War of the 1950s. I chose to give up Latin for it, thinking that a "dead" language was of no interest.

I was placed in a small academic division, "the seven-thirteens," beginning in grade seven and continuing until graduation. We were friends and competitors and regarded as smart nerds. I loved my big high school, with its mix of Italian and Irish Catholics, Protestants and Jews, Armenians, jocks and nerds, vocational and college-bound students. I worked so hard that I graduated first in my class of over 600 students, just as my brother had.

I now realize that I was, in effect, also homeschooled, insofar as Papa and Mommie participated in all facets of my education. Papa saw everything as a teachable moment. On the annual train trips to New York City, he would quiz me on all kinds of topics. I did not object, except for tricky math games, because it felt like a fun television show. At home, Papa supervised my piano practice, cut up fruit to show me geometry, and coached me enough to raise my first C- in seventh grade science to a final A grade. As my official school record was at that point involved, the stakes were high, and my struggle to understand the material much greater. Thus, there were loud voices and tears – and times when I wanted to run out of the room.

On top of that, I went over all my math homework on the phone with girls in the "thirteen" division. And my two best guy friends, Dick and Bruce, came over to do all the required English vocabulary found in the *Atlantic Monthly* – that is, we needed to master every new word in the issue with a definition and use in a sentence.

Mommie became my partner as a student, reading and discussing assigned English novels, looking over my writing, and having me read aloud in Russian. She taught me the trick of preparing work not yet assigned, so I would feel more in control when my teacher introduced it in class.

All this coaching was a blessing and a curse. It was good training and discipline, but in my first year in college, I was insecure and would call Mommie in a panic for help. Papa and Mommie wanted me to overachieve, and I did. Though at the top of my class, I did not make the cut as a National Merit Finalist and my SAT scores were hardly off the charts. So, I knew I was not brilliant like Eddy, and I perpetually worried that I might fail and disappoint my parents. My college friend Kathy Grossman empathized with my insecurity and would comment on our successes by saying, "Well, kid, we fooled them again."

My parents also guided my formal lessons in piano and ballet (photo 17). Mommie would dress up and meet me at school to walk to the bus, and we would travel five miles to downtown Providence, where I had my piano lessons with the young, inspiring Jacqueline Bachand at the Rhode Island Conservatory of Music – and then went on to a small group ballet class.

We would have a snack at Shepherd's Tearoom, next to the department store. I often had a Coke and English muffin or a milkshake and hamburger. The servers wore pale green uniforms with starched white aprons and caps, and the piped-in music was wonderful old standards. We shopped a bit, coming home by bus and then on foot in the dark.

These are the happiest memories of my time with Mommie.

When I got older, it was just piano, with Edna Wood at Brown University, who was known for presenting her students in public concerts and competitions. I loved playing in the school orchestra and always banged out the school song at assemblies. Of course, Papa supervised my practicing at home.

Papa had instilled in me a disdain for sports, except for bike riding. He did no sports himself – he never did – and followed no teams, unlike my friends' parents. The thought of Papa playing golf with Fredda's ever-so-suave father, Archie, strikes me as comical.

My physical exercise included only biking, walking with a destination, and dancing. In high school, I dreaded gym class, which consisted of dodgeball (a scary game), climbing a rope (I never could), and springing over a vault (I never could). However, I loved floor exercises to the theme song of the film *Mr. Lucky*.

In college, we had to pass a swim test for graduation, and play a sport. I could tread water and swim well enough, but my repeated bellyflops for diving were so consistent that the tester said, "Ok, that's it, you've passed." For sport, I opted for fencing, which I had done at YWCA Camp Seaside in Jamestown years earlier and had seemed very much like ballet. Years later, I would address my grandson, Cadel, "*En garde*, I say, *en garde!*" and at age nine he started fencing, as well as French, in my honor.

I never realized that education would propel me to another level of society.

Papa and I first visited the Bryn Mawr College campus during Christmas break of my senior year, in cold and snowy weather. The students had all gone home. The campus was magically still, its gracious old trees covered in snow, its Gothic-style buildings in monochromatic gray, presenting the "Collegiate Gothic" that I would later come to know at Princeton and other universities.

We got into a dormitory (mine would be the oldest, and notable since it had been Katherine Hepburn's dorm) to discover large living areas with working fireplaces for coal-burning fires. And broad staircases with carved banisters leading to wide wood-trimmed halls and rooms with window seats, leaded and wood-framed windows, and plastered walls with hanging rails for posters or corkboards. The library's Great Hall, with its soaring ceiling, lead-paned windows, and rows of wooden carrels with squeaky swivel chairs, was lit only by the small green lamps in the carrels. (The spread of light from those 60-watt bulbs was so limited that we had to move the book around to catch the beam.)

Inspired by Wadham College, Oxford, the outdoor cloistered area of the library, with a fountain in the center, invited the "vita contemplativa" that impressed me. What a change from the three-story brick high school I came from. That environment was bustling and very loud, with shrill bells and intercom announcements, and masses of students in the halls with their polished terrazzo floors and rows of steel lockers banging shut. Even the two private high schools where I later taught were boisterous compared to the quiet monastic feel of Bryn Mawr. It struck me as a serious school.

I know now that its first president, James Rhoads, chose its design in the hope of "elevating standards of taste, giving nobleness to social aims, and promoting living to the highest ends." Given that, years later, my favorite poem would be Charles Baudelaire's "*Invitation au voyage*" ("*Là, tout n'est qu'ordre, luxe, calme et volupté.*"), it is no surprise that Bryn Mawr's setting seemed perfect.

I felt in awe; and strangely, I felt at home. As if I belonged.

At the end of our visit, Papa and I entered Taylor Hall, the administrative and classroom building. An unusually tall and imposing woman beckoned me into her office. It was President Katherine McBride. How regal and formidable she was! I would become so immersed in this ivory tower of academia over which she reigned that in November of my first year, when President Kennedy was assassinated, someone cried out, "The President has been shot!" and my immediate reaction was, "Who would shoot President McBride?"

I must have understood that being among the nerdy "thirteens" all those years, my near-perfect grades, and yes, my constant drilling and coaching at home, had gotten me to that moment. But what I saw and felt that day had nothing to do with studies and seemed distant from my stern, bald factory-chemist father in his heavy overcoat and wool cap. It was tradition, it was excellence, and it was beauty, in the realm of Chopin and ballet.

And this was, for the first time in my life, a door opening to an elite and sophisticated world far from Community Drive.

A critical moment in my college choice – in my overall future aspirations – occurred at a tea to meet members of the New England Scholarship Committee of Bryn Mawr College. The invitation said flatly, "This is not a purely social meeting. It is an opportunity for all members of the committee to meet you personally and none but the most urgent necessity should persuade you to be absent."

We convened in the home of an alumna in Barrington, across the bridge and south of East Providence, a half-hour ride on the way toward Newport. My father drove me and waited nearby. The house was large and elegant, with water views from large windows. The rooms had Persian carpets on hardwood floors and the furniture had a warm patina. I sensed that holding a teacup and saucer plus a cookie would be more than I could manage. I mingled as best I could, mostly aware that I had never been in a home of this refinement and spaciousness. The host was intelligent and gracious. It was a whole new world for me. And I did win that regional scholarship.

Years later, when the girls' school in Baltimore where I taught changed its policy, saying that we would no longer have class parties in big private homes because the scholarship girls might feel uncomfortable, I argued for just the opposite. Because I knew that tea party just across the bridge from Cranston – but a world away – made me determined to emulate both a woman of intelligence and good taste and her reflection in that grand home.

During my first year at Bryn Mawr, 1963-1964, there was so much new and unfamiliar, but I soon settled into the comfort of campus life and grew to love the college's revered traditions.

I was thrilled that real bells pealed to mark class time. Events like Lantern Night, when we sang songs in Greek, with Athena as the patron goddess of the school, and May Day, when we danced around the maypole and then feasted on strawberries and cream, I found especially splendid. On regular days, we ate in our dorm at long wooden tables, mixing with the upper class students at lunch and sitting with our own class at dinner. Black housekeepers in gray uniforms with white aprons served us family-style. Pants were forbidden at dinner, so sometimes we just pulled a skirt over our pants and dashed in.

The same housekeepers changed our sheets weekly, and Black porters stoked the coal fires in our dorm study. I had landed in a world where Black people served (mostly) white Christian girls from (mostly) wealthy backgrounds. This was unfamiliar to me and felt uncomfortable and too "southern." In our class of about two hundred students, there were only a few students of color.

The Lantern Man, who walked us through campus to our dorm in the dark, was predictably white. I do not recall challenging any aspect of this arrangement, but I was relieved when, after my junior year, the system began to change. Self-service was the new protocol, and I had a student job bussing the trays. Where did those housekeepers and porters go?

College offered many opportunities outside the classroom, though I never skipped class. I ventured into Philadelphia on my own for symphony matinees, went to a UPenn-Harvard football game to sit with my Cranston friend Bruce in the woodwind section of the Harvard band, and spent my first Thanksgiving away from home at a friend's house. I met my college sweetheart at a mixer with Haverford on Valentine's Day and frequented the Blue Comet Diner for midnight snacks. When a buzzer signaled that I had a phone call, I would race down the hall, and I would shout "flushing!" when I flushed the toilet so no one would be scalded in the shower.

All but one of my closest college friends were public-school girls on scholarship. They came from across the United States, and we just seemed to find each other. What were the obvious signs of our differences from the private school girls? I immediately realized that the preppies seemed innately confident. They knew that they were academically well prepared and could even coast on that preparation. Also, they were socially at ease. I would catch sight of them knitting complex patterns for sweaters, playing bridge for hours in the "smoker lounge," and nursing Sunday morning hangovers. Their dorm rooms had the best views, and they left for exotic places during spring vacation and came back with a tan. I loved watching it all, though I think I knew I would never be one of them, even if I at first wanted to be.

Bryn Mawr College also lived up to the familiar claim that a small liberal arts college offers its students a close connection with faculty. Professor Marguerite Maurin helped me move up a level in French during my first semester, so that I was able to join her husband Mario's literature survey second semester. The couple befriended me, inviting me to their home, showing interest in my background, and giving me a sense of security and confidence. They later named their daughter Elana, in my honor.

I never knew any swear words other than "damn" and "hell" until I was a first-year student at Bryn Mawr, and a sweet, blue-eyed, blond-haired willowy preppie laid into her boyfriend with a long string of curses that were all new to me – and painfully graphic. I was shocked that a girl with her elegant appearance and sophisticated background could be so coarse. It was startling that this was the young version of that tony Barrington lady of the tea party. And I now realize that I had higher expectations of WASP women. They fascinated me, just as my roommate Renée was fascinated by the seniors – as the Bryn Mawr "sophisticates."

Languages and literature continued to be my favorite subjects. I did a double major in French and Russian well enough to graduate *magna cum laude*. I have a gift for languages, I suppose, a bit like Eddy and his piano. And languages, I had always hoped, would mean travel abroad.

During sophomore year, in 1965, I was accepted into a summer Russian program that was sponsored by the National Defense Education Act and held at Indiana University. We promised to speak only Russian and attend intensive language classes for four weeks, followed by a four-week tour of the Soviet Union. Everything, every day, in Russian. It would prove to be an amazing experience. My parents had not traveled to Europe since the War, and it was a huge privilege for me to do so. I took my first airplane ride, missed a key train connection (with a handful of others) from Finland to Moscow, saw my first mountains (the Caucasus), and experienced the best aspects of communist society at that time, all in Russian.

But even more meaningful was the invitation to spend my junior year in Paris. Following my fencing class in the old Bryn Mawr gym, Kathy Grossman and I met with Professor Maurin. He proposed that we accept an offer to go to Paris on a new program, *l'Académie*, sponsored by Madame Vaudable of Maxim's Restaurant fame and created by her in collaboration with professors from Bryn Mawr and Wellesley. We had been planning to apply to traditional programs, and this took us by surprise, especially since we had never even heard of Maxim's. But the French faculty were "all abuzz" about the program and our sponsorship, so we quickly said yes.

We were euphoric, and it seemed contagious, as everyone marveled at our good fortune – including my parents, who were jubilant. They loved France and could not afford to visit, so this would be a joyous vicarious adventure for them.

Still, the prospect of those two extended trips abroad, plus leaving my boyfriend Bob, so overwhelmed me that I broke out in hives and could not catch my breath.

It was a panic attack.

SS UNITED STATES

à Paris

FIVE

PARIS AND *L'ACADÉMIE* AT MAXIM'S

Kathy's father determined that the cheapest way to get to Europe with a steamer trunk was by sea, so we booked passage on the S.S. *United States,* the largest and fastest trans-Atlantic ocean liner at the time. We were scheduled to depart from Pier 86 in New York on September 23rd, a late start to the school year, and to arrive in Le Havre five days later.

Mommie and Papa came on board with Kathy's family, but only briefly, because I was worried about getting them off in time. I waved at them as they diminished in size in the distance. The music, streamers, and fanfare faded. The 12-story ship was slowly maneuvered, its two smokestacks, each as tall as a six-story building, belching out a deafening sound, but with little smoke. Painted in red, white, and blue, the colors of the American and French flags, and set at a streamlined, raked angle, the stacks alone were a thrilling sight. I felt free, hopeful, and pleasantly excited as we passed the Statue of Liberty.

When my parents spotted Lady Liberty back in 1942, it was undoubtedly bittersweet, as they knew they would not soon be going back to France. For me, it was a moment of nervous anticipation at the prospect of "returning" to my family's home country.

Those five days seemed an eternity of claustrophobia and nausea. Our solution was to be up and outside as much as the rough September seas would allow.

How strange it was that although we were heading to a program run by the most expensive restaurant in the world, we were travelling on the cheap, all alone down on Deck D, where we needed to climb over thick iron thresholds into our tiny cabins, which faced each other and were furnished with only a bed and sink – and no porthole. When the heavy metal doors clanked shut behind us, we were treated to total darkness. I called my space "the vault," since it offered a sense of neither time nor weather.

That first night I never managed to get into the rhythm of rocking in sync with the ship and felt buffeted from side to side. Ugh! So, Kathy and I cleverly decided to stay up as late as possible and sleep on deck during the day. This schedule allowed us to escape our unbearable cabins and nurse our unbearable nausea by avoiding two meals a day. We would go down into the depths at around 4:00 A.M. and, at sunrise, continue sleeping up top, wrapped in wool blankets against the wind and mist of that chilly crossing.

Given that the ship was filled with young Fulbright Fellows, the evenings were non-stop action. These students, all just a few years older, were flirting with each other, and whether they were trying to or not, they impressed me. It was a heady experience, which I characterized in a postcard home as "glitz and glam." An amusing British fellow latched onto Kathy and me, and during the afternoons we three took turns reading aloud sections of the popular sex-satire novel *Candy*. Originally banned in France, it recounts the sexual misadventures of an American girl setting out to experience the world. I had my boyfriend Bob back at Haverford, but these reading sessions seemed harmless, since Kathy and I had concluded this young Brit was gay.

Stepping onto solid ground after so many days at sea, I felt dizzy and disoriented. I was lulled to sleep by the boat train from Le Havre to Paris and then by the taxi to our host's apartment. The world still seemed to go up and down, up and down.

Does everyone remember their first meal in France? I certainly do. It was small and perfectly prepared: an *oeuf au plat* – a simple but exquisite sunny-side egg, soft and a bit runny, and oh-so-different from its dry, overcooked American cousin at Bryn Mawr. Plus, a *tartine* – that is, a simple baguette sliced the long way, with butter and homemade jam. And finally, a huge *café au lait*.

This quintessentially French breakfast was served on my steamer trunk in our bedroom by Aurita, the young Spanish housekeeper of Madame Louyot, who presided in her apartment located at 159 rue de la Pompe. It was on the fifth floor of an elegant 19th-century building in a fashionable neighborhood in the 16th *arrondissement*, on the west edge of the city. Extremely large by French standards (it was half the floor), the apartment housed two other young women boarders, one Polish and one Swedish, who helped defray its cost to the owner, a very circumspect and restrained older widow.

Large and airy, with lofty ceilings, our room had tall French windows opening onto elaborate wrought-iron balcony grates. There was a marble fireplace with a mirror so high as to be useless to someone my size, a large bathroom, a separate toilet, and of course, two single beds.

But these handsome lodgings seemed always to be freezing, which forced us to read our assigned novels under the covers, with one hand poking out to hold our books. Why so cold? Because Madame Louyet was frugal in the extreme. We always seemed to be hungry, too, and Madame must have sensed it, because, when dinner was served, with Aurita reappearing at each course to the sound of a floor buzzer, Madame would say, in French, "This is all that there is, you know."

Much as there had been a disconnect between our fancy ocean liner and life on Deck D, there was now a disconnect between our fancy apartment building and our life on the fifth floor.

At 159 rue de la Pompe I first came to know the mystery of French apartment buildings. When you pressed the buzzer to the side of heavy, oversized double doors, they would swing open to reveal a large courtyard or, as in the case of our building, a lobby with a wide, spiral staircase with a polished brass rail and thick carpet. A concierge lived in a small apartment near the main entrance. She was the then-standard French custodian, who watched the comings and goings of the building, swept the stairwell, maintained the courtyard and its trash cans, and chatted with everyone. Our concierge would sometimes pop out to see who was entering. I liked to think of her as the kind of woman I would read about in a Georges Simenon mystery novel – the one who would read other people's postcards as she sorted the mail and who could be momentarily preoccupied when a criminal might sneak by.

Our posh neighborhood of the *haute bourgeoisie* was residential yet pleasantly busy. I recall the green neon cross sign nearby, indicating a pharmacy, as well as small shops whose windows displayed their entire inventory. Somehow, I learned that it was more agreeable to ask for something specific in these shops, rather than to admit that I was "just looking."

I quickly realized that exact change was valued and big bills not. Kathy and I were both scholarship students and had little spending money. Still, I felt convinced by her that we had no money at all – not a red cent – and that asking our parents for money was a cruel imposition. When I ate alone at a café, I would treat myself to an *omelette avec salade*, but with Kathy, we limited our lunch budget to one franc each (about 20 cents), which typically meant half a baguette, *carottes râpées*, a yogurt, or a piece of chocolate.

We walked for hours each day and were perpetually hungry.

Kathy and I both had cameras, but we rarely used them. Developing film was expensive, and I assured my parents that I had "no desire to record myself in pictures at Maxim's, Versailles, and other pompous places." We never called home; instead, we wrote detailed weekly letters, which became stacks of documents saved by our families. We lived in an expensive neighborhood, 30 minutes away by Bus #63, with its open platform at the back, from the Quartier Latin. I was of two minds: our posh area was safe, quiet, and not touristic, yet it was far from other students and the buzz of bookstores and academic life.

For me, the jewel in the crown of our *quartier* was the large round fountain in the middle of La Place Victor Hugo, best seen from one of the traditional cafés along its perimeter. Women there were always well-dressed, even if in pressed blue jeans with a simple structured blazer and silk scarf, fine shoes, and elegant handbag. I figured out that this must be Parisian chic, and it still is, decades later.

The neighborhood had the most agreeable aromas. Elsewhere, there was the piquant smell of *pissoirs*, where men could enter a metal spiral booth to urinate, in public, with their feet showing. Our elegant square smelled of sugar and butter from the bakeries, as well as of pungent cigarette smoke – Gauloises and Gitanes – and of diesel fuel from the buses. This olfactory mélange was in part why I started wearing classic French perfume, first Guerlain, then Chanel.

Early on Monday, October 4th, Kathy and I arrived for the first time at Maxim's Restaurant – at 3 Rue Royale, near the two monumental fountains flanking an Egyptian obelisk on the Place de la Concorde. There was to be a luncheon, at which we would learn the details of our curriculum and meet our professors. (My souvenir handkerchief, with the jaunty red logo of Maxim's, lists the old-world categories of the lunch menu: *Potages, Oeufs, Poissons, Entrées, Plats Froids, Légumes,* and *Desserts* [photo 18].) Outside the restaurant, the signature red awning with its Maxim's logo sheltered the warm, wooden façade, worn to a soft patina from 70 years of polishing. The windows had elegantly curved frames and were covered with Austrian curtains, the kind with multiple vertical lines spaced evenly to highlight thin bunched puffs. At attention stood a smartly uniformed porter wearing a logo-emblazoned cap.

We were ushered inside. I immediately felt a rush, as if transported to another era, since every element was straight out of *La Belle Epoque* (1890-1914). The atmosphere was warm and intimate – as if it were a hothouse for orchids. A red carpet with green floral design covered the dark floors; ornamental lamps surrounded curvilinear mirrors. The dark woodwork formed smooth curves or complex scrollwork. The glass ceiling in the second room was painted in pale pinks and greens. The banquettes and chairs were of red velvet, and the tables were covered in white damask tablecloths topped with tiny table lamps. Tall leafy plants were strategically placed to achieve an even more lush effect. Large silver buckets held bottles of champagne with Maxim's logo, alongside bronze statuary and flower arrangements.

Nervously, we walked up the wide carpeted staircase in the center of the main room to the loggia, where we waited by the bar for Madame Vaudable. I wrote home that I got "really shook up" when a gentleman earnestly told us that our courses were to be cooking and wine tasting. This seemed so trivial to me at the time. (Now, of course, I would love to have those classes!) As it turned out, he was referring to another program for wealthy European young women, a program already in place at Maxim's.

We were invited to place our drink orders. Madame appeared, a tiny slip of a woman with short red/orange hair, her thin brows arched, her nose crinkled up in an expression of clear if restrained disdain at our choice of the sweet aromatic wine aperitif, Dubonnet. Madame Vaudable was soft-spoken and used subtle facial gestures to show her feelings. She turned out to be most abstemious, her *sole Albert* laid out naked, so to speak, on her plate. She passed on dessert but freely indulged in wine and champagne. I grew to think of her as a Toulouse-Lautrec personality. We secretly referred to her as "Madame Vau doré" ("Golden Calf") and were impressed by her imperious demeanor.

A private banquet room with place cards awaited. I had my first encounter with raw oysters (my letter home noted, "I nearly died eating the slippery things"), pushing most of them under the decorative seaweed. And there was the terrifying moment of the finger bowl with floating lemons when I shuddered to watch Kathy as she toyed with her spoon, fearing she thought it was a bouillon course.

The idea of *l'Académie* was that, in addition to her program in fine wines and cuisine already in place since 1961, Madame Vaudable would now offer a more strictly academic program for young Americans, with only six girls the first year, five from the two supervising colleges (Bryn Mawr and Wellesley) plus one from Randolph Macon. From time to time the elegant and exceptionally bright young heir of a Greek shipping empire, Christine Goulandris, would supplement her courses on food, wine, and fashion by joining us. And a few of the other socialites would sometimes drop in, but they would chew gum and write letters home at the back of the room. This made our professors appreciate the six of us even more – and, we thought, raise their expectations of us all the higher.

Our classes convened in a new building housing the International Union of Railways at 14 rue Jean Rey, near the Eiffel Tower. We took an elevator to a corporate-style room reserved there. The Sorbonne was to be included for just one course, perhaps to academically legitimize this otherwise unusual program. Its monumental amphitheater seated 1,000 students!

A team of cultural luminaries assembled by Madame Vaudable offered our private classes. For a course on the French novel, our teacher Yves Berger, the literary director of *Editions Grasset,* focused on *La Chartreuse de Parme* by Stendhal. I squirm remembering the time he asked us to write a paragraph on the spot in the style of Stendhal; I got flustered and made a mess of it.

We also took a poetry class called *La mission du poète, de Baudelaire au présent,* taught by Jacques Filliolet of the Sorbonne, and a philosophy course entitled *Les pensées occidentales modernes* with Guy-Willy Schmeltz, whose book *Bilan de l'Occident* had just been published.

Madame Vaudable went to great lengths to provide entry into a Russian language course for Kathy and me at *L'École nationale des langues orientales vivantes* ("Langues 'O'"), at 2 rue de Lille. For this, I bought two oversized dictionaries printed in Moscow, one of French to Russian and the other Russian to French, to do direct translations. As challenging as this intimate class was (the very opposite of the Sorbonne), the students would throw spitballs and fool around every time the teacher turned away, a chaos that astonished and amused me.

For a course called *De l'impressionisme à l'art moderne*, we had the dynamic Jean-Louis Ferrier, art critic and journalist at the weekly magazine *L'Express*. Years later, M. and Mme. Ferrier visited my home on Community Drive as they toured New England. I think it was my parents' command of French and familiarity with France that made them more comfortable than I had expected. This professor was passionate about modern art, especially Pop Art in America, and he deepened my own love of art.

Through M. Ferrier, I realized the crowning achievement of that magical year, both intellectually and personally. He assigned to me the work of Jean Dubuffet, a living French artist about whom I knew nothing, and who at that point had no works in museums in Paris. I first saw Dubuffet's paintings at the Galerie Jeanne Bucher at 53 rue de Seine, a narrow busy street with lively cafés and art galleries. Founded in 1925 by Jeanne Bucher, its general director and president was Jean-Francois Jaeger, a charming and intelligent man in his forties.

M. Jaeger took on the project of telling me everything he knew about Jean Dubuffet, a headstrong, anti-establishment artist who had collected enough *art brut* ("outsider art") to form a museum, and who had started painting with no formal training rather late, in his forties. I simply loved all his work, and its varied period styles. I eventually got up the courage to phone a major collector of his works, Jacques

Ulmann, and was invited to see his wonderful Dubuffets in a posh, dimly lit apartment off the Champs-Elysées.

I dove deep into my research, using both my reading of Jean-Paul Sartre's *La Nausée* and what I was learning about Jungian psychology in our philosophy class to describe in French what I saw conveyed in Dubuffet's work: dark existential unease and earthy archetypes.

M. Ferrier was pleased with my paper and, without a word to me, sent it to the artist. I was incredibly surprised to receive a letter from Dubuffet, dated March 21st and sent from Vence in the south of France, thanking me with great praise, inviting me to meet him in Paris the following month, and gifting me a signed drawing in his *L'Hourloupe* style, a bit like a jigsaw puzzle in appearance.

Has any other moment in my academic life been better?

I met Dubuffet in the elevator on the way to a special dinner hosted by the Parisian collector M. Ulmann. Dubuffet expressed surprise at how young I was. At dinner he railed on about the materialism of the museum world and argued for bartering art. We joked about that, after I offered him the shoes off my feet for an artwork. The evening flew by. I knew at that moment that art and its history were to be part of my life forever, writing to my parents, "It is Russian I feel obligated to, French I have been prepared for, and art that I love."

Another unique feature Madame had conjured up for her *Académie* was a series of encounters with distinguished guests, for which we would carefully prepare. It had never occurred to me that as members of *l'Académie* we would be lunching regularly at Maxim's. Madame Vaudable offhandedly invited us, using the French grammatical negation "*ne...que*," which was new and a bit confusing to me. "*Puisque vous n'êtes que six...*," meaning "Since there's but six of you," she arranged for us to have lunch with her and a special guest every

Friday at noon. We suspected that the guest of the week was chosen as much for Madame's pleasure (and ego) as for our edification.

The first lunch featured the aging François Mauriac; in preparation, we read four or five of his novels, on top of our normal classes. Next came the young conductor/composer Pierre Boulez ("dynamic, brilliant, charming," I wrote home), for which a music critic had prepared us, prior to an evening black-tie concert of the *Rite of Spring* at the Opera, which we attended. Then there was the niece of Marcel Proust, whose apartment with oval rooms overlooking the Seine we later visited. Le Corbusier's recent death meant a visit by his disciples and a trip to two of his architectural gems. We expected to meet Jean-Paul Sartre himself, but each weekly syllabus came and went without his name appearing. This was a disappointment for me, having put myself squarely in the category of Sartrean Existentialism that year. I came to believe that man created God, and that humans both enjoy and suffer from their freedom.

Still, Madame had the power to open so many doors for us. Museums were available to our art history class during off-hours. We also participated in field trips that were already in place for the "finishing school," such as going with Madame to the presentation of the spring collection at the headquarters of Dior at 30 avenue Montaigne and having a well-known guide take us around the monumental Chartres Cathedral.

The weekly lunches at Maxim's, waiters hovering over and smoothly darting in and out by our table with Madame, were distinguished by a demanding, even exhausting, need to multitask with focus: eating the best food I had ever eaten; drinking either a top champagne or grand cru wine; listening to the older "éminences grises" who spoke in very rapid French; mustering up the courage to say a few intelligent words or ask a question in correct French; and taking in the atmosphere, people, and fashion of the room. (Madame Schiaparelli is at the next table!)

The cuisine, so refined and well proportioned, begged repeating, and I would go on a jag for weeks before moving on to a new dish. I stuck with a form of roast beef for weeks, until Eddy insisted that I try other main dishes. Happily for me, the final banquet of the year, on June 7th, featured fried sole in mustard sauce followed by rib roast "du Charolais" (the finest beef in France comes from the region of Charolles) with Yorkshire pudding, Maxim's potatoes, buttered string beans, and seasonal salad. Plus, of course, a luscious dessert.

As is characteristic of French cuisine, it was often the sauce and the side dishes that made it all so delicious. The delicately painted Limoges cup with lid concealing chocolate mousse was a marvel. The strawberry version of a Napoleon was so tall it was hard to be neat with a fork. The way we simply fell over the food must have looked comical. We always had three full courses with champagne or wine.

What followed each Friday lunch? A rush to class, 30 minutes by metro. We debated: taxi or metro? The metro required a transfer in the long, gritty, and hot underground walkways at Châtelet. Taxis were costly, and we needed two for the six of us. But either way, class would last two hours on Friday afternoon, right after our two hours of feasting, with champagne making us giggly or wine making us drowsy.

It was a fairy-tale life, and it sometimes bordered on the absurd. For example, on one spring weekend, Madame took us to Reims, in the Champagne region, specifically to taste champagne at the Château de la Marquetterie. We stayed in town at the venerable Hôtel du Lion d'Or, and did of course visit the renowned Reims Cathedral, but an introduction to champagne production was paramount. The fancy printed invitation to a dinner at the Taittinger estate had come to us via Madame Vaudable's personal secretary, the flamboyant and beautiful Madame Boyer, whose exaggerated tone of voice, dramatic hand gestures with long bright fingernails, heavy makeup featuring huge eyelashes, and puffy blond hair with highlights made her a taller, fuller version of Madame.

Her attached letter concluded, "Attention: You will partake in numerous tastings of champagne, and you risk getting a little too silly if you overdo it." (Kathy and I read carefully, as we were unaccustomed to drinking.) We enjoyed an elaborate dinner featuring three types of champagne, thus three fluted glasses for each of us, which made for a table littered with glassware! We played silly games organized by our hosts, the owners of Taittinger. Our Bryn Mawr classmate, Sally Newell, won a magnum of champagne just for having worn the shortest skirt. (We drank it with chocolate cake two months later, to celebrate Sally's 21st birthday, playing *Cadavres exquis*, a surrealist word game that we found could be poetic or risqué.)

As I wrote to my parents, "Except for the cathedral, it was a useless trip. I'll chalk it up as a negative lesson." Though I now wonder: Was I simply being an intellectual snob?

Other special occasions seemed perfect. Kathy and I each received two tickets to a black-tie gala at the Palais Garnier featuring Stravinsky's *Rite of Spring*. I invited a Fulbright Fellow from the transatlantic crossing, a Haverford alum whom, decades later, I saw again in his Chicago apartment, when he was the departmental host for a visiting guest – namely, my husband Gary. And there was the premier of the *Ballet Roland Petit* at the Théâtre des Champs-Elysées, with set and costumes by Niki de Saint-Phalle, Jean Tingly, and Martial Rays. This time I used my elegant invitation to the beauty salon of Alexandre Jeunes Filles et Harriet Hubbard Jeunes Filles at 120 Faubourg St.-Honoré, which stated that I could come for hair and make-up needs at a special rate of $4 (about $40 in current dollars) during 1965-1966.

The second and only other time I used that invitation to Alexandre's beauty salon (I, too, had become frugal in the extreme) was for a cocktail party at Maxim's, attended mostly by stuffy old men in tuxedos, which was staged as a prelude to an invitation to a debutante ball. Yikes! I was not at all interested in being a debutante, which I held in absolute disdain, as I did sorority life.

Overall, though, I felt like Cinderella at the ball. I had made the round trip back to France for the Klausner family in grand style.

In all those months of 1965-1966, I never once wondered who had been dining at Maxim's during the War, only one generation before me. Questions like that – and especially questions relating to the actions of the Vichy regime – were not yet being asked in France. No one at any time mentioned World War II to us, nor were we savvy enough to ask any questions.

I have since learned that Maxim's enjoyed protected status during the Occupation to provide the German High Command with fine dining. That is where Hermann Göring chose to eat when he came to Paris to oversee the seizure of art from Jewish collectors and dealers in the nearby Jeu de Paume. Göring's favorite Berlin restauranteur, Otto Horcher, took over operations of Maxim's for the duration of the War, and the Vaudables stayed on with their staff. For this, the French resistance closed Maxim's after the liberation, but it reopened two years later, in September 1946.

All I remember noticing then was how young and naïve we six members of *l'Académie* were against the backdrop of that old-world red velvet nest. Did I ever wonder about the wartime role of the Hôtel de Crillon, right around the corner from Maxim's, which I much later learned was the headquarters of the Grand High Command, housing Nazi generals from June 1940 until Paris was liberated in August 1944? Could I have imagined that just down the street from our lovely apartment at 159 rue de la Pompe, at number 180, was the site of a notorious Gestapo torture chamber? Is it possible that Madame Louyot did not know about it? I doubt it.

Yes, I came "back home" to France in 1965, 23 years after the Klauzner family fled. But what was the home I came back to?

While I was living in the glamorous world of *l'Académie* and the rue de la Pompe, I was simultaneously living in a second world that year – one much closer to my world in Cranston and nourished by the spirit of Vilna. I was a frequent guest of my parents' leftist cousins Boris and Sonia Grinberg, who lived in the heart of the Latin Quarter – which would explode in student protests in May 1968. Boris was a French-born nuclear physicist who, as a member of the French Communist Party, was denied entry to America to visit my parents. His wife, Sonia, who was born in Vilna, along with their daughter, Martine, about my age, offered a vastly different intellectual and social world from that of *l'Académie*.

I would regale the Grinbergs with tales about Maxim's over weekend lunches in their simple apartment. Delectating over my portraits of people and accounts of the menu, demanding ever more details, they would, at intervals, throw up their hands in shrieks of laughter. I especially loved to poke fun at the formidable and suave Count Benoît de Boigne, age 26, whom Kathy was dating. We had been invited to his parents' château in Normandy and were amused to discover that he addressed his own parents with *vous*, the formal, distant, cold version of *tu* or "you." We had magically been transported back to the 19th century! Sadly, Count Benoît died in 1970 at the age of 31 after crashing his Bugatti on the Champs-Élysées.

The Grinbergs were fun, direct, probing, and intellectually serious – and bohemian. It was they who introduced me – and Eddy, who had come to Paris for a short visit – to the Marais, the old Jewish Quarter. They drove us there in their vintage black Citroën for a typical Jewish lunch at a tiny deli, the kind with windows full of pickle jars and vats of herring. This was a gritty ethnic neighborhood before it became today's gentrified and expensive tourist destination. And a world away from Maxim's. I saw a new side of Paris that was Jewish, and I liked it very much.

I was the Grinbergs' guest at many avant-garde performances and theater productions by Jean-Paul Sartre and Eugène Ionesco. I waited three hours in line with Boris, Sonia, and Martine to attend an *Homage à la poésie russe* at the Maison de la Mutualité, featuring ten Soviet poets, Anna Akhmatova among them, with translations provided by iconic French literati, including poet Louis Aragon. The excitement I felt in the packed hall was feverish.

My perspective on the Soviet Union and communism was enriched and my sympathies deepened. My parents spoke Russian at home, I studied Russian at Cranston High East, and I had been bold enough to utter the phrase "better red than dead" during a classroom discussion of the ongoing Cuban Missile Crisis in the fall of my senior year – for which I was verbally pummeled. I had spent four weeks in the Soviet Union prior to going to France and had seen the achievements and disappointments of their system.

Yet it never occurred to me during any of those conversations with the Grinbergs to ask Boris if he was the one who gave my father money when he pedaled in from La Rochelle just after the German invasion – though I now believe that he was. Or later, to quiz Martine, who could have helped fill in the blanks. Time is critical, and I waited too long to contact Martine, who was like a sister to me that year.

During a recent trip to Paris, I finally followed up on a little address card with Martine's name that I had kept for decades. Martine's apartment was not far from our Airbnb in the Marais. Anti-government protests over raising the mandated retirement age were then raging in the nearby Place de la République. It was late afternoon on a beautiful spring day when we found what we believed to be her apartment building. The building had five stories and a shiny blue door, but there was no list of occupants outside. I was convinced that someone would soon enter or exit, so that we could slip into the entrance hall and survey the buzzer list for her name and apartment number.

We waited no more than five minutes, and someone did come out: Martine! Gary and I both recognized her at once, after 50 years, but she did not recognize us. She was vivacious, engaging, and friendly – but her mind, when it came to anything specific about the past, including my name, was a blank. Martine's daughter, Judith, later told us that her mother was suffering from a "*maladie neuro-degénérative*" of recent onset.

I now realize that the Grinberg apartment was the home I had come back to in France. The Grinbergs were a version of the Klauzners, if they had never left France, with Martine standing in for me. I never chatted disparagingly about those odd old leftist Jews over oysters and champagne at Maxim's; it was the other way around. Just two months into the fairy tale, I wrote a scathing review of all things rich and chic in the life I was now (in part) living in France.

> *I just saw two Ionesco plays – ABSURD! This whole expe-*
> *rience, if you ask me, from the l'Académie to the boat to*
> *luncheons once a week at Maxim's to the coiffure I had done*
> *at Alexandre's for a cocktail party at Maxim's, which had*
> *stuffy old rich men and chicly dressed young women, to my*
> *age of 20 this Sunday, to the invitation to come out at the*
> *Debutante Presentation – to all this – I say, a toast, to the*
> *cult of the ABSURD!*

A few weeks later I offered a brutal response to Mommie's enthu-siastic endorsement that I "come out" with European debutantes.

> *The very idea is painful that I can "keep up with the best*
> *of them." What does this <u>keeping up</u> mean? And who is the*
> *best? Who are <u>they</u>? … It's disgusting, and frankly, tho your*
> *intentions are good, I'm surprised at a lack of critical mind*
> *in your judgment of fun. ...*
>
> *Also, I quite dislike so far the pomp people, those who*
> *frequent Maxim's; I must be a peasant at heart.*

This was the girl whose parents came from Vilna talking. This was the liberal who was curious about Russians, the Soviet Union, and student demonstrations. This was the immigrants' daughter from Community Drive.

The contradictions of my delight in and disdain for the Maxim's lifestyle are now clear to me. True, my year *chez l'Académie* elevated my aesthetic sensibilities; nevertheless – though I would not have admitted it then – I was still Kukla, the little "Doll" of Izia and Niuta.

SIX

MY JOURNEY TO PONARY

This has been a tale of two journeys. The first, Papa's, was ever west-ward, beginning in 1923 when he crossed the Rhine to Strasbourg and the land of *liberté, égalité, fraternité*. Then continuing, after the War broke out – and now with his small family – into the French free zone and then, in 1942, through a combination of ingenuity, courage, and good luck, on to safety in America. Papa was driven onward by seeth-ing antisemitism and ultimately, by the threat of death at the hands of the Nazis. He and his family finally found their home, in Cranston, Rhode Island, in 1948.

The second journey was mine, driven not by someone else's hate, but by what Papa said hate can never take away, namely, education. My childhood dream of returning to my family's home country of France became reality in 1965 in a most unanticipated and spectacular way, at *l'Académie chez* Maxim's Restaurant, thanks to my years of study, and my gift for languages – which I inherited from my parents.

And finally, in 2004, as I approached my sixtieth birthday, I began a third journey, which was a journey of discovery, driven by my desire to know, and ultimately to tell, my family's story.

The Jewish city within a city that was Vilna between the Wars no longer exists. But in 2004 I read about ongoing reconstruction, in the post-Soviet era, of the Jewish Quarter. At that moment, I realized that at least some of its distinctive buildings and narrow byways had likely escaped the destructive power of the Nazis and the Soviets. And it dawned on me that I needed to see Vilna for myself. For so many years I had thought of my parents as being from France, when, really, their story began in Vilna. Thus, I applied for the inaugural year of the Birgit Baldwin World Studies Faculty Prize at Roland Park Country School, where I had been teaching for 20 years, in order that I, with Gary and our daughters Nicole and Sonia, could visit Vilna and other key locations associated with the Holocaust. Ultimately, I won the award.

Our journey began in July 2005 in Berlin, where we walked along the broad avenue Unter den Linden and visited the Olympic Stadium, where huge Nazi parades and rallies had taken place. How many documentaries start with footage of those rallies, with their swastika-emblazoned flags, goose-stepping soldiers, and the shrill voice of Adolf Hitler? Now I saw a quiet and green city, and noticed how people would wait for the green light to cross an empty street. Was this a sign of a German obedience to rules and authority? We entered the restored Great Synagogue, built to hold 3,200 congregants, which was heavily damaged on Kristallnacht, the "Night of Broken Glass" – November 9/10, 1938 – when more than 1,400 synagogues and 7,500 Jewish businesses and homes were attacked.

To think that in 1937 my father had walked those same streets and sensed the growing antisemitism all around him, and that in April 1938 my parents had married and were living just over the border in France! Perhaps my father's uncle in Germany – the one who "waited too long," hoping to sell his business – was a victim of Kristallnacht.

In the former Jewish Quarter, we encountered a memorial sculpture of an oversize table and chairs, one knocked over to symbolize the violence of Nazis barging into a home and dragging the family out. And we kept nicking "tripping stones" (*Stolpersteine*), shiny brass memorial pavers set in the sidewalk slightly above grade to catch the toe of your shoe and thus your attention. Each is inscribed with a name, age, and date and location of death, as an everyday reminder by the German artist Gunter Demnig that nearby there once lived a person or family deported to a concentration camp and murdered. (There are now thousands of tripping stones across Europe.) One example is the Schneebau family: Father Hermann, age 37; Mother Jenny, age 35; Daughter Thea, age 12; and Son Victor, age two. One shiny square reads: "Here lived VICTOR SCHNEEBAU / Born 1941 / Deported 1943 / Auschwitz / Murdered."

We also saw a memorial titled *The Missing House* by the French artist Christian Boltanski which lists the names and professions of deportees on the side of the building where these Jews had lived. Of course, all these addresses are known because the Nazis were meticulous record keepers. Every detail, no matter how horrific, was documented.

Nearby, a monument marked the spot where Jews were collected and walked to the Grünewald train station. Loading platform #17 at that station has a commemorative iron grate along the track, with dates and the number of Jews deported on each of those dates, as well as their destination at a death camp. For example: "27.3.1945 / 18 Jews / Berlin – Theresienstadt." Small stones were piled up at both the collection spot in the city and at the iron grate of the train station, a practice kept at Jewish cemeteries, where visitors place stones atop tombstones. Like flowers, the stones show that someone has been there for remembrance and reverence, but as stones they symbolize permanence. I was in the habit of bringing stones from the Rhode Island beaches loved by my family to set on my parents' Lincoln Park Cemetery tombstones. (My mother had died in 1991, my father in 1993.)

Later that day, we visited the large Memorial to the Jews of Europe by the American architect Peter Eisenman, whose hundreds of tomb-like stelae made of concrete with anti-graffiti coating (made by the same company that had made the Zyklon B gas pellets used in the death chambers) rise from an undulating, disorienting ground line. Walking between and among them in so many directions and with so many varied angles had a numbing effect, broken only by my dismay at the sight of teenagers lounging around on the blocks and jumping between them. Like myself as a younger person in Paris, they were likely unaware of the history and solemnity of this space.

But the most chilling visit for me was our trek to Wannsee House, one hour from Berlin. I was even more unnerved there than when the local train from the Paris airport stops at the suburb of Drancy, the town where all Jews were rounded up for deportation in 1942. Or when I was flummoxed by how close Dachau is to Munich, and Auschwitz is to Krakow.

Wannsee is an elegant lakeside villa, a magnificent mansion built in the style of an Italian country house. There, at the Wannsee Conference on January 20, 1942, 15 high-level Nazis sat around a table and made a momentous and unprecedented decision in just two hours. The world knows that over the centuries Jews were found and gathered in ghettos and were fully expelled from a country, as from Spain in 1492. But now arose the new idea of straight-out extermination: "The Final Solution." Could these 15 men really have been from the same stock as Bach, Beethoven, and Brahms, the three great "B composers" whom I had been raised to love?

Germany has done much since the War to acknowledge its past and educate its children. Still, I was stunned by Wannsee. I was shocked by one display panel that showed a man in a hat and raincoat who could have been my father. He is reading *Der Stürmer* – just as my father had described himself reading that antisemitic newspaper on the streets of Berlin in 1937. I wonder: What was this man thinking as he stood there?

Next was Dresden, that jewel-box city of art that was all but destroyed by American and British bombs near the end of the War. There we visited the German Hygiene Museum, with one particularly disturbing section on eugenics. This exhibit, showing stereotypical studies of various ethnic groups, was used as part of Hitler's "scientific" theory of why the Nordic race was superior.

Then we left for Poland, to the great city of Krakow, where we saw a once-defiled Jewish cemetery that had been restored and a synagogue showing Nazi film footage of Jewish children carrying chairs for school in their move to the ghetto, where they faced slow starvation, typhus, and tuberculosis. I felt sick at heart.

The following day at Auschwitz I felt even more troubled. The Nazis had documented and saved everything. Whatever were they going to do with the seven tons of hair found boxed up when the camp was liberated? Heaps of suitcases, piles of shoes, rooms of eyeglasses and prosthetics – what, I wondered, may have belonged to my father's uncle and his wife? But worse was my realization that 75% of those arriving at nearby Birkenau went straight to the gas chambers, with Jews in charge of the crematoria for three months before their own execution. How could they live with themselves? The layers of collaboration for survival were unpeeling.

Who could dream up Cell #20, the "suffocation room," where 30 to 40 prisoners a night died, or Cell #22, the "standing cell" with no windows, where four out of 12 inmates had to stand all night in one position before going to work? And the mass toilets, in a world of dysentery. The remains of endless blocks of brick buildings seemed to me like an archeological dig. It was July 23rd, and it was 41 degrees, with a brief dusting of snow. I bought boiled wool mittens.

I felt more prepared to visit Vilna, a short flight away with Polish Lot Air. But our daughter Nicole was not ready. She was distraught and depressed. We left her and Sonia in the comfort of the Krakow hotel and flew on our own, with the determination to see my parents' hometown, and the hope of probing further what my heritage means to me.

That is, we hoped to discover some of the physical world that shaped my parents' lives. Tomas Venclova's *Vilnius* city guide was useful, but what was essential to our quest was the two-volume *Jerusalem of Lithuania: Illustrated and Documented*, published by Leyzer Ran in 1974, and passed on to me when my father died. It includes thousands of images of people, buildings, street life, documents, and events, thematically organized, that attest to the long and rich history of Jews in Vilna. My uncle Israel wrote one of the introductions.

Not only do those volumes bring Jewish Vilna back to life, but they also offer specific clues to my parents' lives, thanks to the meticulous annotations that my father added. On page 247 of volume I, for example, there is a small arrow pointing to the man in the back row on the right in a group photo of the managing committee of Poale Zion in 1934. A sheet of paper tucked in after page 1 tells us this is my mother's brother Kolia. The most interesting and useful page for our trip, though, shows a photo that indicates where my father and his family moved in 1914 – the corner of Gitke Toibes and Lidska Lanes (photo 19). In the Old Town, near a nunnery, I recall my father saying.

We arrived in Vilna in perfect weather during the last week in July to discover a beautiful city, friendly people, and interesting if not great food, including their national dish, *cepelinai*, a potato dough dumpling stuffed with pork.

We were surprised that the Jewish Quarter was easy to find and remarkably intact, including signs in Hebrew painted on the walls of former shops. So, the matchups with images from Leyzer Ran's book should have been easy. (Communism, as we discovered during our academic year in Romania in the mid-1970s, is exceptionally good at unintentionally preserving the past.) Yet we were puzzled that we could not find my father's apartment building. After all, we had the address and the clue about a nunnery. But all the street names had been changed, maybe more than once. And none of the local religious sites seemed to fit. We knew, though, if we found that low arcaded wall shown in the printed photo, we would be at his building.

Our breakthrough came on day three, when we visited the Green House (Holocaust Museum) and there, by good luck, met its founding director, Rachel Margolis, who happened to be paying a brief visit from her current home in Israel. (Gary knew her on sight from having read an article on the Green House in *Smithsonian Magazine*!) Rachel was a lively, engaging woman who reminded us both of my mother – so we at once bonded. She was excited to learn that I was related to the famous Israeli historian Joseph Klausner, whose picture and brief biography were posted on a nearby wall. And she was especially taken with my father's diploma, which she all but insisted must be added to her display. (She had to settle for a photocopy.) And to my amazement, Rachel knew all about my mother's all-but-mythical cousins, Misha and Grisha, the two Vilna brothers who survived the War by hiding out in the sewer system. In fact, she proudly showed us a little diorama of their great hideout arrangement (they appear sitting at a table, eating), where their sewer line was represented by a length of black garden hose.

As for the Klauzners' 1914 apartment, that was easy. Rachel pointed out its current street address in our guidebook and laughed about the nunnery idea. Not a nunnery, she said, but the oldest church in the city, dedicated to Saint Nicolas. It was just a short walk away: There was the low arcade wall and there was my father's very handsome apartment building (photo 20). Its courtyard sheltered a large lilac tree, which suddenly reminded me of the lilac tree in the back yard of our Cranston house. That eternally scrawny tree that my father for years struggled to keep alive. This could be no coincidence.

We also learned the address of Rasha and Kolia, from a list compiled by the Nazis when they rounded up the Vilna Jews. They, too, lived in Old Town, just a short walk south of the original Klauzner apartment, off a courtyard. In this case we had an apartment number, so we knocked. But no one answered.

There was an added bonus. Rachel told us that my father's high school was now the national art conservation and restoration center, and that it was just a few hundred yards from the Radisson Hotel where we were staying. And here, a truly odd coincidence: The evening before, we had dinner at the wonderful Beer House & Craft Kitchen with a young couple we knew from Baltimore, Yunhui and Paul Singer. Yunhui was a former Mellon Conservation Fellow at the Walters Art Museum, and her husband Paul had recently joined the diplomatic corps, with Vilnius as his first posting. Ironically, from the terrace where we ate, we could almost see the Church of Saint Nicolas, which was just a few blocks away. And when we took a stroll after dinner, we unknowingly passed in front of Rasha and Kolia's courtyard.

Yunhui was volunteering three days a week at the conservation center, which I was determined to enter and explore. I explained to the bewildered young woman who answered the door that I wanted to meet with our Walters friend.

"Not here today," she said.

But I pressed on, explaining that Gary was the museum director where she had previously trained, and that he was very keen to take a quick look at where she now worked. In we went. The air was suffused with the smell of school, one that is so familiar to me. Sunlight from oversized windows bathed the beautiful rooms, with tall ceilings and wide staircases leading to more beautiful spaces. It was easy to imagine my father among the rows of students immersed in learning. At that moment I felt close to him, even though he had left these halls more than eight decades earlier.

Our most important stop – and by far the most disturbing – was at a site known as Ponary, a forested summer recreation area about seven miles south of the city. Over the summer of 1941, 21,000 Jews from Vilna were murdered there, most shot and buried in mass graves. By the end of the War, upward of 70,000 had died there.

Ponary was chosen by the Nazis for mass murder because it was close to a railroad line and because a year earlier Soviet troops had dug huge pits there for the storage of oil. As we approached the pits, with their various memorial monuments, I was struck by two things: profound silence and the sweet smell of pine.

We were alone.

I had learned from Nazi records displayed at the Green House that my aunt Rasha was forced from her apartment into one of the two ghettos set up near the Great Synagogue in early September 1941. According to the Yad Vashem database of those murdered in the Shoah, Rasha died at Ponary on September 12th. And according to the list of family members my father compiled in the 1970s, all but one of the other members of the Spokoiny clan died sometime in 1941, presumably shot at the Ponary oil pits.

There is a small museum at Ponary with a few scraps of personal items belonging to the victims – watches, belt buckles, razors. In 1943, as Soviet troops advanced westward, the German command forced Jews from the ghetto (organized into "corpse units") to dig up the Ponary bodies, stack them on wood, and burn them. They then ground up the remains, mixed them with sand, and reburied them.

All of this, to cover up the Nazis' horrendous war crime. I felt shame and guilt: shame that Jews had carried out the orders to extinguish their own people, and guilt that I had survived the loss of a whole family I didn't even know and had never before truly mourned.

More than a million died at the concentration camp of Auschwitz, in many more ways and in far greater numbers than at Ponary, which was simply a place of mass shootings. Nevertheless, I was struck by how little remains at Ponary, and how little attention those remains receive. As if the Jews of Ponary are the orphaned dead.

And all the while, I could not get out of my head the belief – the conviction – that Mommie's family was in the soil beneath my feet (photo 21).

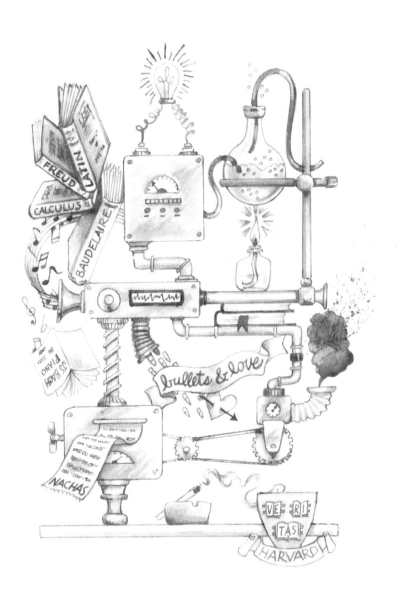

SEVEN

THE SURVIVORS, THE VICTIMS

Six million Jews perished in the Holocaust. Among those who survived, some prospered, and some were forever damaged. The stories of their children are mixed; for certain, I was one of the lucky ones.

There is no question: I got to "go home" to France in high style for having been raised in America. In the post-war world of Eisenhower optimism, sprawling housing developments, a vast new web of interstate highways, and shiny cars. I was raised in a land of upward mobility. Of multiple versions of the American dream, where the daughter of Polish-Jewish immigrants could grow up to rub shoulders with old-money WASPs in the ivy-covered Gothic halls of a private college. And then sail off to Paris and *l'Académie* at Maxim's.

I wanted to be 100% American and, thanks to my nurturing parents, hard work, and some good luck, I succeeded.

My choice of a husband is part of that story. I met Gary Vikan in a summer class at Princeton in 1968 (photo 22), where we tried to split up the homework for two years of Latin in six weeks. After we lived together in my tiny Princeton dorm room for several months, it was time for Gary to meet Mommie and Papa.

We arrived in the evening. I do not recall that Papa said much; I know he went to bed early. Mommie, though, was agitated and wanted to talk.

"Then, you killed us with bullets; now, you kill us with love."

Her lament, invoking the end of the Jewish people, came at about 2:00 A.M. and pretty much summed things up. I don't recall responding and, in any case, this was a monologue and not a conversation. Gary, I could tell, was shocked.

Eddy had eloped with a Catholic of Polish descent, and now they were confronted with a Scandinavian Lutheran.

When we visited my Israeli relatives in 1971, one of my aunts remarked on how well Gary spoke English. The Israeli Klausners had somehow come to understand from their American brother that Gary was from a Norwegian farming family. Well, they weren't so far off. His grandfather, Knut, arrived from Norway in the 1870s and eventually homesteaded with his wife, Birgit, in the Turtle Mountains of North Dakota. Franklin, Gary's father, was the youngest of their 11 children and the only one to earn a college degree – in journalism, from the University of North Dakota.

In 1937, Franklin married Wilma, a first-generation Swede from Grand Forks, whose father was a butcher. She was the second-to-oldest of seven musically gifted sisters. For 50 years, from 1938 to 1988, "Frank" Vikan published the weekly newspaper in Fosston, Minnesota, a town of about 1,500 in the northwest part of the state. He and Wilma raised five children, of which Gary was the youngest.

Hope Lutheran Church was a big part of his family's life, as Temple Beth Israel was a big part of my family's life.

Gradually, my parents warmed up to Gary, as they had warmed up to Eddy's wife, Kathy. My father was especially taken with Gary's thesis topic, which focused on the art of the Jews of Late Antiquity. In June 1970, just before Gary and I left for a study year in Europe, we raised a glass of Chartreuse with Mommie and Papa in their tiny kitchen to celebrate our forthcoming (post-Europe) marriage. And Gary's conversion to Judaism; Mommie's late-night "bullets and love" lament had left a strong impression.

What drew me to Gary? Well, as noted in Chapter Three, as a child I had simply adored the television show *I Remember Mama*, the story of a large, loving Norwegian immigrant family, including the blond son, Nels. I often hummed the theme song, by Edvard Grieg. As also noted in that chapter, I had carefully cut out the blond, pink-cheeked Campbell Soup Kids I found in my mother's women's magazines and pasted them into a scrapbook. To me, Gary looked like the boy in *I Remember Mama* and the Campbell Soup Kids.

Raised in the heartland of America, Gary came from a big family, which I envied. He made me laugh, loved to cook à la Julia Child, and made the best cappuccino in town. Plus, he was an art historian and keen to travel. He was brilliant but down to earth – "from the sublime to the ridiculous," I have always said. And he was as American as apple pie. I am sure that he represented something that I was after, namely, a quintessential American. And, more basically, escape from a Jewish immigrant home.

We have been married for over 50 years.

Papa worked for more than three decades as a factory chemist – in Hagondange, the Vichy free zone, and Providence. His true calling and joy, though, was teaching, which defined his public life (photo 23). Papa taught Hebrew most of his adult life, and math and sciences as a substitute teacher for 20 years after he retired from the electric company at age 65. He was a dedicated and gifted teacher, with scores of devoted students. Laura Jacobs, a student from one of his Hebrew classes, wrote in 1984 (when Papa was 81) to "My dear Mr. Klausner."

> *You have always been a grandfather to me. … You have taught me everything about Hebrew that I will ever know. You will always be in my heart when I go to college until my last day. … I can't help telling you how much you mean to me.*

Papa's scrapbook has many such notes from his students and their parents, especially after a big 1986 *Providence Journal* article about what one student called his "heroic escape." Another student remarked that she had learned chemistry, but, through his stories of the war years, she had learned much more.

Papa's zeal for teaching was not confined to the classroom; he was intent on teaching all metropolitan Providence with his many opinion pieces in the *Providence Journal*. These began in the 1960s and reached a peak in the 1980s, when he was in his eighties. In 1988, the year of his near-fatal stoke, Papa wrote at least nine articles, including one titled "Between Life and Death," wherein he chronicled his stroke and later hospitalization.

Papa's topics usually centered on his family's war experiences, Israel, or Jewish life more generally. His style was thoughtful, simple, and direct, and he was not afraid to criticize Israel (for its treatment of Palestinians) and American Jews (for getting nose jobs). After having looked back at Papa's early life in Vilna, I'm convinced that he picked up his comfort with politics and polemics from the energized Jewish life of debate he had experienced in his youth.

One of Papa's last submissions to the *Providence Journal*, in late 1988, bears the title "Teacher's Creed."

> *I never thought of myself as a deep thinker, but I had the chance to expose young minds to the values of life. … I would tell of my life in Europe and America, of World War II, of my travels on bicycle, of concentration camps, of learning English, and I was excited to see the children get interested and involved. … I loved my work, and I loved my students.*

Would Papa have fared better in France? Perhaps not. He would likely not have had the opportunity to teach so many students and to write so many articles for the newspaper. Might he eventually have moved our family to Israel, as his brother Misha had done (his son became a rabbi)? I don't think so; Papa made his final decision in 1936 when his parents and three of his siblings emigrated to Palestine. He had instead already chosen France as his new home, I suspect because of values he absorbed as a teenager in his gymnasium: Yiddish and a European future for Jews, as distinct from Hebrew and a separate homeland. The Bund versus Zionism.

In 1991, after Mommie died, Papa agreed to go into a nursing home. We were lucky to find a small, simple facility in East Providence, which he seemed to like. But since Gary and I felt he should be near us, we secured a spot for him in the specifically Jewish facility associated with Baltimore's Sinai Hospital, no more than 15 minutes from our house. We thought he would enjoy our more frequent visits and the company of other Jews, as well as the on-site religious services.

Papa, though, had other ideas. He hated his new surroundings and his unfamiliar caregivers – and so his stay lasted exactly 24 hours. Back up to Providence he went on a plane with his walker, to familiar surroundings and friends. His roommate was the father of his beloved doctor, Walter Thayer, a national expert on gastrointestinal diseases and, even better, a professor at Brown Medical School. My father had gone back home.

Papa died two years later, in March 1993, at the age of 89, from a stroke. It was his second; his first stroke, in August 1988, had nearly killed him and left him physically weak. He was disciplined in his therapy and fought for life as long as he could. I admired his strength, and I set out to become the rock of my own family through his example.

Overall, Papa made out well in the United States, belonging to his community in a meaningful way. He pushed through, survived, and thrived. But I wonder: If Papa had not been a stranger in a strange land, an immigrant by force and not by choice, might he have been less demanding of Eddy?

In 1965, Paris buses still had seats reserved for the war wounded – the *Blessés de Guerre*. Most were obvious, as they were missing limbs or had been blinded. Only much later did I learn that there were wounds of war that could not be seen.

Papa ended his newspaper article "Remembrance…" from 1979 – the one in which he described the murder of relatives and friends at the hands of the Nazis – with these words: "The psychological impact on those who lived through this period is beyond description." Whom might he have had in mind – who were those psychologically "wounded in war"? Perhaps his own wife, and his son.

I have no doubt that Mommie would have fared better had our family remained in France. She was a European at heart. When my parents began to travel abroad, in the 1970s, she was truly at home. But for her, nostalgia for city life, where she could walk to cafés, markets, and small shops, was clouded over by her acute sense of loss.

In France, Mommie would have had familiar outlets for spending her days, but in Cranston, she had no one else, so she lived vicariously through me. As far back as I can remember, Mommie loved to dress me nicely (photo 24). I grew to love hats and shoes, which completed my elaborate outfits. My childhood saddle shoes evolved into adult spectator shoes, my eight-year-old's round hat into my current collection of felt, fur, and knit winter hats as well as straw summer hats of all shapes. Mommie sewed my ballet costumes by hand and made outfits for my Ginny Dolls, using parts of a mitten and scraps of felt to make an ice-skating skirt, hat, and sweater for the doll.

At home, Mommie was a sociable woman who smiled and laughed easily, with a giggle that made her shake. She wore the kind of leisure wear once sold in stores in the housecoats department: that is, fleece or cotton zip-up robes in neon colors for winter and pale flowered patterns for summer – with little white socks and low-heeled sandals. This was vastly different from her snappy appearance in public. The only photographs I have of her in her house outfit are all from much later, when she was in her sixties and seventies and seemed no longer to care. Earlier, she refused to be photographed that way.

Mommie had prided herself on her physique in her early years. She loved to recall how the crowd on the train airlifted her petite self overhead until she sighted little Eddy. She would also reminisce about her beauty and popularity as a young woman, saying, "I was like this," holding up her pinky finger to show how thin she had been. And like Jack Benny, Mommie habitually fudged her age; she was in fact six years younger than Papa, but on my birth certificate she claimed to be ten years his junior. This led to some ambiguity about the month and day of her birth, which I finally verified in researching this book. Mommie was in fact born on December 12th, but she chose instead to celebrate her birthday on Simchat Torah ("Torah Celebration"), which typically falls in October.

Mommie did not seek salon haircuts, manicures, or the other luxuries that my friends' moms sought. I saw her as a loner, cloistered in our house, except to take me to lessons and shopping, or to visit a few friends in Providence – plus the great annual pilgrimage to New York City. I felt, even as a child, that she was living through me, reading the books I was assigned, going over my Russian homework and even my English essays, dressing me up with care, and making friends with my friends.

She did not seem visibly anxious, except for one habit: she would pick her lips until they bled.

Mommie had every reason to be depressed and feel hollow, as the Nazis had murdered every member of her immediate family – her parents, brother, and two sisters – as well as aunts, uncles, and most cousins, and her friends. She never seemed to me bitter, just sad, poring over her photo albums and romanticizing her happy days before the War, back in Vilna, while sitting in our tiny kitchen in her housecoat, with her unkempt hair.

Mommie created her own universe at home. People came to her, especially my friends during and after high school. No other mother that I knew held court like she did, sitting in her neon bright housecoat in the evenings with my friends, especially the boys, Jewish and not. They loved her questions, her curiosity about them, her undivided attention, and her listening skills. I, too, could confide in her. She was eager to give me advice on my love life, my schooling, and, of course, my outfits. And she was usually right.

When I was a senior in college, my artistic Jewish boyfriend had the idea of taking time off from Haverford to live with the Lubavitch community in Williamsburg, Brooklyn. During that period, I was exploring my relationship with Judaism; the previous summer I had spent time in Israel on a kibbutz, which I loved. So, I decided to spend a weekend with a Lubavitch family in Brooklyn to see what he was getting into – which might be what I would be getting into as well. The large Hasidic family with whom I stayed was kind and hospitable, and boisterous in their joy. But their ritualistic behavior and synagogue service unnerved me. Coming from a women's college, I found the distinctions between men and women – their enforced separation in temple, the feverish dancing of the Hasidic men – shocking. I wrote all this to Mommie and have saved her reply, in which she offers opinions about my boyfriend, whom she knew well.

> *My dearest Kukla*, it begins, *He is only a talker, not a doer. He lives in a cult of absurd – not you.… His dreams are about different things that always center around him. He rarely does anything about it, he just changes the dream. … I do believe that you are in love with a dream.*

That same year, 1967, as I was applying to graduate school, Mommie again gave me savvy advice, this time on universities: "California is fine," she said, "but too far away and, by the way, the Haverford type would prefer Berkeley, plus Stanford has a great standing and more ambitious boys. Try Yale anyway, what can you lose? About Princeton – it is getting more interesting, and maybe you should try there, too."

Then she launched into questions about a Manet exhibition at the Philadelphia Museum of Art. "Try to see it," she concluded.

And finally, on to my new black dress. "What shoes? Maybe you should buy silver sandals, or your suede black shoes?"

Wow, in some respects I'm exactly like my mother; that is, this could be my two daughters and me, right now.

Mommie died in June 1991 of a heart attack, at home, at the age of 81. She was cared for in her last months by Alma, my parents' elegant caregiver, who otherwise made her living by modeling for Hallmark's Mahogany greeting cards. Mommie and Papa adored Alma, and when the house was sold, Papa insisted that she take as much of their furniture as she could use.

Mommie was disturbingly passive during her last days. Frustrated, I would beg her to roll over in her bed, or sit up, and she would hunker down into her blanket and say, "Leave me alone."

I still sing all the French children's songs Mommie sang to me as a child. My three grandchildren, Cadel, Thorsten, and Bodhi, have all heard *Au clair de la lune* many times, as if in Mommie's voice.

So, yes, she lives on.

Eddy was a special case; simply put, he was a genius, but a profoundly troubled one (photo 25). He was equally gifted in the arts and sciences, winning awards all through school in both areas. I called him "Sparky" after the popular children's record album *Sparky's Magic Piano,* in which the piano would play beautifully with no effort from little Sparky. Eddy could play without sheet music – any tune, in any key, and in any style. It dazzled everyone.

In high school, Eddy played Beethoven's Concerto No. 3, with his teacher playing the orchestral part on a second piano, before an overflow crowd at the Rhode Island Conservatory of Music. I recall being squeezed into a tiny slot in a stairwell leading up from the main floor.

I remember Eddy as teasing but protective; my childhood friends say he was unique in treating his little sister's friends kindly. My friend Karen says that she saw him as a "golden boy." My happiest moments growing up centered around Eddy: playing with the train set, trying to fish in Roger Williams Park, and, above all, playing the piano, with "Name That Tune," four-hand pieces, and singing to jazz and show tune favorites. And hearing hours of his practicing the most difficult pieces in the classical repertoire.

We also loved watching TV with a full box of chocolate chip cookies and milk.

When Eddy went off to Harvard at age 17, I was enormously proud but missed him terribly. I wrote to him every day. When he said that was not necessary, it was even excessive, I was hurt and stopped altogether.

Was this the first sign that something had changed?

Eddy did well at Harvard, majoring in chemistry. His classes were fine, though his days of straight A's were over. He played piano for the Hasty Pudding Club, served as the coxswain of his house's rowing crew, played billiards, admired his friends, and seemed happy. But in the second semester of his senior year, Eddy failed a chemistry class and had to complete it and get his degree over the summer. The whole turn of events was a dagger in our family's heart, and it meant that his medical school options would be limited.

Papa attributed Eddy's academic failure to "playing billiards too much." But as I learned much later – and as none of us at the time recognized, or chose to recognize – Eddy was then experiencing, at age 20, his first mental health crisis. Was a pattern beginning, in which he was unable to cope with stress? Was his psychic structure so shaky that it would collapse at moments of transition?

While at the University of Pittsburgh Medical School, Eddy met Kathy Lenn, who would become his wife. Shortly before they married, he experienced a second and more severe mental crisis involving short-term loss of vision in one eye and sudden numbness in a hand. His doctors saw these as symptoms of multiple sclerosis, though Kathy maintained they were psychosomatic.

After his residency at New York City's Mount Sinai Hospital, where he had a successful stint as chief resident, Eddy and Kathy eloped in June 1966. Eddy let our family know via a Western Union telegram, "Kath and I were just married this morning and very happy, kisses and love." It seemed so impulsive.

I was devastated that I did not meet Kathy until after their wedding; I felt left out and jealous. We were all stunned to learn that Eddy's new wife had been briefly married before, had never graduated from college, and was a lapsed Catholic of Polish descent. Mommie *hated* the Poles, who, she said, "spit on us."

Mommie and Papa were shaken by Eddy's behavior. Papa threatened to cut Eddy out of the family and any future inheritance. I was petrified by the prospect of losing my brother, and I wrote home from France, during my junior year at Maxim's.

I feel sick about the situation of our family. [But] *If non-Jews destroyed your family, Mommie, then it is equally so or even worse, for you yourselves, because of non-Jews, to split apart our family.*

It's the present and future that count; the past too, but primarily for what good one can draw out from it..... I am skeptical of Eddy and sad for him, but he is my brother and we four are the only family I really feel I have.

Somehow Papa relented, though Eddy did not: He had the audacity – the cruelty – to ask for a German-made Volkswagen for a graduation present from medical school. And he got it! My friends were astounded, and so was I.

Remaining in New York City, Eddy opened a private practice in psychiatry. Soon, he was busy with referrals from his former Mount Sinai colleagues. Meanwhile, Kathy began working her way up in the fashion industry. She was smart as well as beautiful, a great cook, and a gifted home decorator. Kathy loved Mommie and Papa, and they ended up accepting and admiring her. The marriage produced no children and, with both Eddy and Kathy struggling to establish careers, there were endless high-pitched squabbles over chores and money.

I always assumed that Eddy chose psychiatry in part to understand himself. I would like to believe he was asking the same questions I was: Why did he go out of his way to disappoint and offend his family? Why did he taunt Papa by repeatedly saying, "I'm not your *nachas* machine!" (*Nachas* is Yiddish for pride producing.) On the contrary, Eddy had become our family's source of unending *tsuris*. (*Tsuris* is Yiddish for aggravation and woe.)

Soon, Eddy's life started to unravel. His ensuing mental turmoil, in the early 1970s, was overwhelming, including three psychotic breakdowns in three years, with talk of suicide, each ending in a locked ward.

Gary and I stayed with Eddy at his country house outside Katonah, New York, for a few weeks after his third episode, in the summer of 1973; I would drive him into the city to see his doctor, while Kathy worked and his best friend covered his practice. Our main job, though, was suicide watch; the point was to keep Eddy away from his New York City apartment, which was on the 16th floor.

My brother's chronic depression was punctuated, when he was hyper, by paranoia and an explosive temper. A misunderstood word or phrase during casual dinner conversation and Eddy was out the door, shouting, into the dark of night. This was especially disturbing when he and Kathy were staying at that grand, isolated country house on a small gravel road.

This paranoia and those outbursts led to years of alienation from Papa and, to a lesser extent, from my family and me. Eddy was simply unpleasant to be around. He had become increasingly bossy and argumentative, as if he were aspiring to be a sourer version of Papa. Ed's ("Eddy" had been abandoned) time had now become "precious," and so if I wasted it, I was in for a severe scolding.

Like Papa, Eddy was preoccupied with famous relatives, no matter how distant. (For Papa, every noteworthy Klausner was either an "uncle" or a "cousin.") The most eminent was Joseph Klausner, whom I've referenced in earlier chapters. He was born in Vilna a generation before my father and was a major proponent of reviving Hebrew as a spoken language. While attending my father's "dream university" in Heidelberg, he took part in the first Zionist Congress in Odessa and, after the Russian Revolution, emigrated to Palestine. Joseph Klausner became editor of the *Encyclopaedia Hebraica* and, most impressive to me, authored important books on the history of Christianity: *Jesus of Nazareth* and *From Jesus to Paul.* He was also a candidate to be the first president of the State of Israel. Although his bid was unsuccessful (Chaim Weizmann won), even his loss was something for Papa and Eddy to brag about!

Joseph Klausner is described by his great nephew, the celebrated Israeli author Amos Oz, in the memoir *A Tale of Love and Darkness.* The author's name had been Amos Klausner, but at age 15, when his mother committed suicide, Amos rebelled against his father's world and changed his name to Oz, the Hebrew word for courage.

Eddy was particularly captivated by Amos Oz and wrote him a rambling letter in 2005, which reveals his damaged psyche. (I found a copy of this letter when I went through Eddy's papers after he died.) The letter starts, "I am the worst kind of person you can imagine. Living in the middle of nowhere, you probably think no one will come and visit you unless they come from Germany to give you a prize. Yet I might." Eddy goes on to explain that he bought Oz's memoir, highlighted it in yellow (obsessively covering *every* word), and then typed parts to e-mail to his sister (me). He must have seen himself as a stalker, since he concludes by promising Oz, "I would never harm you, nor your family. … And I did not kill your mother, even indirectly."

Eddy underwent decades-long treatment with an eminent psychoanalyst – and decades-long use of lithium to stabilize his mood swings. While it helped, it also ultimately led to kidney failure. Besides bipolar I disorder, Eddy's medical challenges included coronary bypass surgery, a kidney transplant, and, finally, full-blown multiple sclerosis.

And it didn't help that he smoked three packs of Old Gold Straights a day.

Along the way, Eddy's psychiatric practice collapsed, and he and Kathy drifted apart, eventually divorcing after years of separation. It now amazes me that Kathy stuck with him so long.

Papa was wonderful and patient with his students, but I do not recall that kind of patience with Eddy, upon whom he put intense pressure to excel. He could be very unpleasant – sharp and severe. His manners were limited, from a crisp answering of the telephone with "Klausner here," to pushing away a dinner plate because of "those red things" (pimentos). I saw him use a belt on my brother's early teen backside. Papa did not want to accept that my brother had deep psychological problems, though I recently learned from Kathy that Papa made a trip alone to New York City to visit Eddy in the psychiatric ward.

For me, it's difficult to escape the conclusion that Eddy was among the millions of the *blessés de guerre* of World War II. And I suppose this was only to be expected. Scores of scientific papers have been written on the psychological impact of war – and of refugee status – on the lifetime mental and physical health of children, beginning with post-traumatic stress disorder, depression and anxiety, and even multiple sclerosis.

Mommie often told the story that when Eddy came to America after two years on the move with my parents, he would go to sleep clutching pieces of soft white bread.

I see my brother as a shooting star – spectacular, and then fading, mortally wounded.

Eddy died penniless in the locked ward of a nursing home in the Bronx in October 2013, at age 74. I was alone with the funeral director at his burial in Lincoln Park Cemetery, not far from our parents' graves.

His epitaph reads simply, "A Brilliant Pianist."

CONCLUSION

I recently revisited Maxim's Restaurant and sat at the spot where our little troupe of American college juniors met for lunch each Friday (photo 26). Fifty-eight years separate that visit from my first visit to those rooms, in October 1965.

I started this quest two decades ago. After my trip to Vilnius, I told the tale of my family's harrowing escape from Vichy France in an upper school assembly at Roland Park Country School, under the title, "Stories My Father Told Me." I then wanted to expand this short narrative into an essay or perhaps even a book, a project that grew more compelling when I realized that my college year in Paris as a member of Maxim's *Académie* was, in effect, my family's return, in poetic triumph, to the land they loved but were forced to flee.

I have learned much along the way.

From my childhood onward, I had a vision, born of Mommie's talk of her "premonitions" that guided their flight from danger in wartime France, that Mommie, Papa, and Eddy were constantly on the move, on bicycles, one step ahead of the Nazis. In drafting this book, I came to realize that they were not in moment-to-moment danger. For 18 of the 24 months that separated the German invasion of France in

June 1940 from my parents' departure for America in May 1942, Papa was employed in the free zone, first as part of a mining operation, and later in a steel mill in the small industrial town of Decazeville. The Klauzners lived in a handsome building on the town's main square, at 1 Place Wilson, just opposite the monument to World War I. And my brother Eddy, plump and happy, was the subject of a fancy studio photo, taken in nearby Rodez.

Only very recently did I put two and two together: Papa worked in a Vichy regime steel mill that was in the service of the Wehrmacht – much as, I suppose, Maxim's Restaurant and its owners were in the service of the Wehrmacht. That dark, sticky word "collaboration" has taken on a new meaning for me. I realize that in wartime, every family does whatever it must to survive. Collaboration was even the ugly truth for those Jews who filled the cremation ovens with other Jews to prolong their own lives.

This raises another question that never crossed my mind until recently: What would have happened to the Klauzner family if Uncle Gustave did not exist? What would have been their fate if they had no entry visa to the United States and had to stay on in Decazeville?

I knew even as a child that the Nazis exterminated the Jews of Vilna, with more than nine out of ten falling victim, including all but one of Mommie's family. But in France, three out of four Jews survived the Holocaust. No other country has a comparable record. That figure is especially striking given the active role that the thoroughly antisemitic Vichy regime played in helping the Nazis with their roundups – a truth finally acknowledged officially in 1995 by French President Jacques Chirac.

My family's experience gives clues to that high survival figure, even for the Jews in France who were not French citizens. First, there was the network of sympathetic Jews, including the Kane family, who took my mother and little Eddy in when they were evacuated from Hagondange; the Grinbergs in Paris, who helped Papa when he needed money; and the lawyer named Levi from the phonebook in Marseille, who arranged to have his daughter produce an official translation of Papa's forged document.

And second, there was the kindness of strangers who were not Jewish, including the photographer in Rodez, who produced an official-looking copy of Papa's forged document, and, especially, the young woman behind the desk of the Marseille police station who, despite being told by Papa that the document before her was forged, nevertheless procured an exit visa for the Klauzners. And don't forget that crush of passengers on the overnight train from Decazeville to Marseille, who passed Mommie "like a ball" over their heads so she could find Eddy.

Papa's circumstances were vastly different from those of his uncle with the pharmaceutical factory in Germany, who had been deported with his wife to the concentration camp in Gurs – and from there, on to Auschwitz and death. While not a French citizen, Papa had been in France for nearly 20 years, had a work permit, and held a critical position in a critical industry. Nevertheless, what Papa knew of the fate of the Jews in Vilna and of his uncle and aunt's circumstances in Gurs quite naturally created the conviction that he and his family were caught in a life-or-death predicament. Thus, the enormous risk Papa took in presenting a forged document to the officials in Marseille.

But much as my parents' French-Jewish cousins, the Grinbergs, survived the War in France, my parents and Eddy would likely have survived as well. So, Cranston might instead have been Decazeville, and Maxim's *Académie* would not have been part of my life.

How did I come to author this intergenerational story? Especially given my lifelong reluctance to write, my sense that I never really learned how to write well, and the fact that I gave up my Ph.D. dissertation at 100 pages, after having edited every sentence multiple times?

Many factors have played into my new sense of motivation and capability.

For one, I started the piano again after decades, with lessons, when I inherited a spectacular baby grand from Eddy following his death in 2013. For most of my adult life I resisted playing the piano, but I felt an obligation to Eddy to make use of that fine instrument. It turned out to be pure pleasure, with effort but immense joy.

Maybe, I thought, writing could come more easily now too, and bring satisfaction.

By good luck, I am, like Papa, a natural born teller of tales. As I thought about my happy years of teaching French, Russian, and the history of art at Roland Park Country School, I realized that what my students really valued and what kept their attention were my stories. Mementos I'd bring to class and good old-fashioned travel slides kept their focus as I would spin my yarns.

In French class, I would pull out a wispy blue sheet of airmail writing paper from 1965, sent to me by Madame Vaudable at Maxim's Restaurant, and talk about my Cinderella-like year in Paris at the age of 19. I'd tell the tale of my first lunch there, when none of the six of us college kids in *l'Académie* at Maxim's knew what to order from the upstairs bar while we awaited our host, Madame Vaudable.

One girl said, "Dubonnet," and we all followed suit.

When Madame appeared, she asked, "What *are* you drinking there?" She sniffed and turned up her nose at the answer.

I never drank Dubonnet again.

Then, as I typically did, I offered my students a life lesson. I said, "When you get older and don't know what to order for an aperitif, you can never go wrong with a *coupe de champagne*."

They listened attentively.

Weaving stories and life lessons into teaching academic content was what I had learned from Papa.

Throughout my quest, I have been looking to find answers – to fill in the blanks of my family's story. It shocks me when people don't seem interested in knowing their own family history. Especially my Jewish friends, whose families have often had to struggle to survive.

I believe that everyone has a story, and a good one, if told with honesty and conviction.

Yet, I put "Stories My Father Told Me" aside for 20 years.

As noted earlier, in his seventies, at about the age I am now, Papa started to send articles chronicling his war experiences to Providence-area newspapers, which were eager to publish them. Why did he choose to reveal his life story to the world at that age, and why have I decided to tell my story just now? I'm not sure, but it is certainly no coincidence.

Of course, I have had doubts: Would anyone care? Thankfully, Gary turned out to be an enthusiastic editor, and our two daughters, Nicole and Sonia, eagerly awaited each draft.

But how about the world out there? Will anyone besides my family and a few childhood friends care to read *Finding Home*?

I'm beginning to think so. I was recently at a dinner party, and the guest next to me, who makes his living in marketing, said, "Tell me what you're all about."

Without thinking, I replied that I am the product of the Holocaust, as my parents managed to get out of France one month before the first comprehensive roundup of Jews for deportation to the camps. I am, I said, the archetype of the American dream, and have had an amazing and happy life.

He replied, "This is what we call 'a hot start.'"

1. Isaac Klauzner and his father, Hayim; Vilna, early 1920s

2. The Spokoiny family; Vilna, 1912

Аттестатъ Зрѣлости

Виленской еврейской смѣшанной гимназіи

С. М. ГУРЕВИЧЪ

съ курсомъ и правами мужскихъ гимназій.

Предъявитель — сего ученикъ восьмого класса Виленской еврейской смѣшанной гимназіи С. М. ГУРЕВИЧЪ, *Клаузнеръ Исаакъ Хаимовъ Шебселевъ,* какъ видно изъ документовъ, вѣроисповѣданія іудейскаго, родившійся *1 Іюля 1903 года* поступилъ въ означенную гимназію въ *седьмой классъ* по свидѣтельству за пять классовъ *Виленской еврейской Реальной гимназіи при Обществѣ Просвѣщенія Евреевъ (ОПЕ)* и по испытаніямъ за *шестой классъ* и, находясь въ ней до окончанія полнаго курса ученія, въ продолженіе всего этого времени былъ поведенія *отличнаго.*

3073/2

3. Isaac Klauzner's high school diploma; Vilna, June 1921

4. Anna Spokoiny and her boyfriend, Volodia; Vilna, 1937

5. Isaac Klauzner and Anna Spokoiny, with siblings and friends;
Vilna, 1930

6. Anna Spokoiny; Vilna, June 1937

7. Anna Spokoiny with Isaac and Moses ("Misha") Klauzner;
Metz, August 1937

8. The extended Spokoiny family; Vilna, April 1938

9. Isaac and Anna Klauzner; Nice, February 1939

10. Isaac and Anna Klauzner, shortly before Eddy was born; Hagondange, France, July 1939

11. Gurs concentration camp; Near Pau, France, 1941

12. Isaac, Anna, and Eddy Klauzner; Ceilhes-et-Rocozels,
Vichy France, June 1941

13. Isaac, Anna, and Eddy Klauzner; Nîmes, Vichy France, April 1942

— 1 —

FRANCE
TITRE D'IDENTITÉ ET DE VOYAGE
N° 23

Nom du titulaire : KLAUZNER

Prénoms : Isaak
Lieu de naissance : Kawa - Eraki (Pologne)
Date de naissance : 13 Juillet 1.903
né de : Chaïm
et de : Rachel Kapilovitz
Nationalité : ~~Polonaise~~ N^{le} Apatride
Profession : Ingénieur chimiste
Résidence de fait : Decqenite (Aveyron)
Résidence antérieure : Hagondange (Moselle)

Le détenteur du présent titre n'a pas qualité pour obtenir un passeport français.

— OBSERVATIONS —

14. Isaac Klauzner's altered *Titre d'Identité et de Voyage*; Marseille, May 1942

15. Anna and Elana Klauzner; Queens, summer 1946

16. The Klausner family; Cranston, 1953

17. Elana Klausner; Cranston, 1956

18. Maxim's Restaurant handkerchief; Paris, April 1965

Corner Gitke Toibes and Lidska Lanes

Угол Гитке–Тойбес и Лидского переулков

ראָג גיטקע־טויבעס און לידסקע גל'

פינת גיטקה טויבס וסימטת לידסקה

**19. Church of Saint Nicholas and the Klauzner apartment building;
Vilna, before World War II**

20. The former Klauzner apartment building; Vilnius, 2005

21. Elana Vikan with our tour guide; Ponary, Vilnius, 2005

22. Elana Klausner and Gary Vikan; Princeton, 1969

23. Isaac Klausner; Warwick, 1981

24. Anna and Elana Klausner; Providence, 1953

25. Isaac and Eddy Klausner; Cranston, late 1970s

26. Elana Vikan in Maxim's Restaurant; Paris, 2023

THE FAMILIES

The KLAUZNERS, all born in Troki, near Vilna

1872   Grandfather Hayim (d. Israel)

1875   Great Uncle Gustave (d. U.S.)

1886   Grandmother Rachel (d. Israel)

1902   Aunt Genia (d. Israel)

1903   My father Isaac ("Izia") (d. U.S.)

1904   Uncle Israel (d. Israel)

1907   Aunt Sarah (d. Israel)

1909   Uncle Moses ("Misha") (d. Israel)

1910   *Aunt Rashel ("Rasha") (d. Vilna)

The SPOKOINYS, all born in Vilna

	*Grandfather Osher (d. Vilna)
	*Grandmother Chaya (d. Vilna)
1899	*Aunt Sonia (d. Vilna)
1906	*Aunt Lisa (d. Vilna)
1907	*Uncle Kalman ("Kolia") (d. Vilna)
1909	My mother Anna ("Niuta") (d. U.S.)
	*Killed by the Nazis at Vilna/Ponary in 1941

THE TIMELINE

1903 through 1937

July 13, 1903   Isaac Klauzner is born in Troki

December 12,
1909   Anna Spokoiny is born in Vilna

1914   The Klauzner family moves to Vilna

1921   Isaac graduates from high school

1926   Isaac graduates from the University of
Strasbourg

1927   Isaac takes a job at the steel mill in
Villerupt, France

1929   Isaac takes a job at the steel mill in
Hagondange, France

1936-1938   Anna is courted in Vilna by Volodia

1937   Isaac visits his uncle in Germany and
sees a Nazi parade

| August 1937 | Anna visits Isaac and his brother Misha in Metz |

1938

April 24	Religious double wedding of Isaac and Anna, and Kolia and Rasha, in Vilna
August 13	Civil wedding of Isaac and Anna in Hagondange, France
November 9-10	Kristallnacht ("Night of Broken Glass") – Nazi pogrom targeting synagogues, and Jewish businesses and homes

1939

February	Isaac and Anna honeymoon on the French Riviera
August 4	Edmond Klauzner is born
September 1	Germany invades Poland
September 3	France and the United Kingdom declare war on Germany – World War II begins
September 5	Anna and Eddy are evacuated to Riom, France

1940

| January | Isaac is briefly reunited with Anna and Eddy in Riom |
| June 6 | Isaac flees Hagondange in advance of the German invasion |

June 14	Paris falls
Summer	Isaac, Anna, and Eddy are reunited in La Rochelle, France
October 3	The Vichy regime passes the *Statut des Juifs,* drastically reducing the role of Jews in French society
Fall	The Klauzners, including Misha, move to the "free zone"

1941

January to July	Isaac is employed by the mining operation in Ceilhes-et-Rocozels, free zone
June 22	Operation Barbarossa – Germany attacks the Soviet Union
July to May 1942	Isaac is employed by the steel mill at Decazeville, free zone
Summer and Fall	Nazis kill 40,000 Vilna Jews, including eight members of Anna's family and one of Isaac's sisters
1941	Isaac visits his uncle and aunt who were deported from Germany to the concentration camp at Gurs, France
December 7	Japan attacks the United States at Pearl Harbor
December 8	The United States declares war on Japan
December 11	The United States declares war on Germany

1942

1942	Isaac's uncle and aunt at Gurs are deported to Auschwitz and killed
March 19	The Klauzners, including Misha, receive their travel identity documents in Rodez
April 17	They receive their entry visa to the United States in Marseille
Late April	Isaac learns of a new Nazi order that citizens of those countries at war with Germany cannot leave France
Late April	Isaac forges a document saying he is no longer a Polish citizen
May 8	Isaac presents that forged document to a woman working for the Marseille police – then confesses
May 12	Isaac returns to receive his exit visa from that same woman
May 13	The Klauzners, including Misha, sail out of Marseille for Morocco
June 7	They sail out of Casablanca for New York City
June 25	They arrive in New York City
July	They travel by train to Uncle Gustave Klausner in St. Louis
July	Isaac takes a job in Spokane, Washington

1943 and later

March 1943	Misha joins the U.S. Army
July 1943	The Klauzners are living in the Bronx
June 6, 1944	D-Day – Allied troops invade Normandy
May 8, 1945	Victory in Europe (VE) Day
1945	The Klauzners are living in Queens
October 24, 1945	Elana is born
1947	Isaac receives his master's degree from New York University
Early 1948	Isaac takes a job as chief chemist at Narragansett Electric in Providence, Rhode Island
Early 1948	The Klauzners move to 91 Wheeler Avenue in Cranston, Rhode Island
November 1948	Isaac and Anna become naturalized U.S. citizens and change their name to Klausner
Early 1953	The Klausners move to 33 Community Drive in Cranston
Fall 1956	Eddy goes to Harvard University
1957	The Klausners get their first car
1960	Eddy graduates from Harvard

1961	Eddy goes to medical school at the University of Pittsburgh
1963	Elana graduates from Cranston High School East and goes to Bryn Mawr College
Summer 1965	Elana goes to the U.S.S.R. as part of intensive Russian language program
September 23, 1965	Elana and Kathy Grossman sail out of New York City for France
October 4, 1965	Elana has her first meeting of *l'Académie* at Maxim's Restaurant
October 1965 to June 1966	Elana is a member of *l'Académie* at Maxim's in Paris
June 1966	Eddy and Kathy Lenn elope
September 11, 1971	Elana and Gary Vikan are married
June 1991	Anna dies in Cranston
March 1993	Isaac dies in Cranston
2005	Elana wins the Birgit Baldwin Prize at Roland Park Country School, Baltimore
July 2005	The Vikans travel from Berlin to Vilnius, exploring sites associated with the Holocaust
October 2013	Eddy dies in a nursing home in the Bronx

ACKNOWLEDGEMENTS

I am deeply grateful to Tracy Gold, editor and author, for her insightful review of my first draft, including guidance for the overall structure of the book, and its title. For the last draft, I sought the expert wisdom of another local editor and author, my friend and former student, Elisabeth Dahl, who offered superb editorial advice as well as many creative suggestions. And to neighbor and friend, Katherine Murphy, I owe special thinks for her "catches" in the final proofreading.

My deepest gratitude goes to my inner circle of friends and to my family, who together jumped in with important questions, numerous corrections, their own memories – and unfailing moral support. My pal since childhood, Dick Honig, a practicing psychoanalyst, generously shed important new light on my brother Eddy's emotional struggles. A boatload of love and thanks goes to my dear college chum, Kathy Grossman, Victor Hugo scholar and former French professor at Penn State, for years of devoted friendship, her stack of letters home from Paris, her vivid memories of long-ago events that remained a bit hazy for me, and her unfailing clarity of thought. My deepest thanks go to Fredda Brennan, gifted artist and designer – and my very best friend from childhood – for immediately agreeing to become my partner in this quest, through her brilliant illustrations and cover design.

Fredda also has a terrific memory and great stories to tell about our youth. Placing my absolute trust in her was easy.

And a special thank you goes to my long-time friend Kathy Lenn, retired Senior Vice President/Creative Director at Vogue, Butterick, and McCall's Pattern Company, who generously shared her warm and vivid memories of my parents as well as of her former husband, my brother Eddy. And to my cousin in Paris, the eminent translator Anne Rabinovitch, for insights into the lives of my parents' French relatives during the War.

And now, for my family. Profound thanks to my daughter Nicole, a former assistant D.A. in Manhattan who now owns her own educational consulting business, for her skilled, intelligent, and ever-encouraging editing of my second draft. And to my daughter Sonia – who proved to me that miracles can happen – whose gift of humor and unbounded enthusiasm buoyed me throughout this literary voyage. The collaborative effort that is *Finding Home* owes its existence to the creative direction and remarkable memory of my husband Gary Vikan, Byzantinist, museum director, author, and public speaker. Gary got me started on my Birget Baldwin Prize application in 2004 – with its resulting trip to Vilnius – and it was when he finished his last book, and agreed to work with me on this one, that I finally got down to serious writing. Without Gary's keen interest in researching my parents' photographs and documents, I could never have reconstructed their amazing story.

In the end, it is to my "growing up family," Anna and Isaac Klausner, a.k.a. "Mommie and Papa," and my brilliant brother Eddy, that this book belongs. For it was their lives that were so brutally shaped by the Holocaust.

THE TEAM

Elana Klausner Vikan (left) was born in Manhattan, raised in Cranston, Rhode Island, and educated at Bryn Mawr College, with a double major in French and Russian. She spent the summer of 1965 in a Russian language immersion program and trip to the Soviet Union under the National Defense Education Act, after which she studied in Paris for her junior year. At Princeton University, in the Department of Comparative Literature, she was awarded the Sibley Prize to support a research year in Paris. Elana was a lifelong teacher of French, Russian, and the history of art, working at Princeton University, Georgetown Day School, and, for 28 years, Roland Park Country School in Baltimore. Elana now spends time with her family and three grandsons, plays classical music on the piano, enjoys her Boston Terriers, and continues to travel extensively throughout Europe, though most often to her beloved France, with her husband Gary. She collaborated with Gary on the book *Postcards from Behind the Iron Curtain*, about their year in Romania in 1974-1975.

Fredda Kapstein Brennan (right) was raised in Cranston, Rhode Island, and graduated from the Rhode Island School of Design, where she majored in painting and illustration. She spent her senior year in Rome, as part of the European Honors Program. In San Francisco, with her husband, Tim, she made an animated film that was shown at the San Francisco Film Festival. In New York City and then the Hudson Valley, Fredda designed printed textiles and paper goods for design companies including Brunschwig & Fils, Wathne, P/Kauffman, Caspari, and Vera Bradley. Her work involved travel to France, England, Japan, and Korea. Fredda now spends much of her time drawing and painting, and occasionally participates in group exhibitions. Her website is freddabrennan.com.

Gary Vikan was director of the Walters Art Museum from 1994 to 2013; from 1985 to 1994 he was the museum's chief curator. Before coming to Baltimore, Gary was senior associate at Harvard's Center for Byzantine Studies at Dumbarton Oaks. A native of Minnesota, he received his B.A. from Carleton College and his Ph.D. in the history of art from Princeton University. Gary was appointed by President Clinton to his Cultural Property Advisory Committee, and has debated twice on the topic of antiquites repatriation at the Oxford Union. He was knighted as a *Chevalier des Arts et des Lettres* by the French government in 2004. In retirement, he lectures, teaches, and writes. His recent books include *Sacred and Stolen: Confessions of a Museum Director* (2016); *The Holy Shroud: A Brilliant Hoax in the Time of the Black Death* (2020); *My Father Took Pictures: Growing Up in Small-town Minnesota* (2021); and, with Elana, *Postcards from Behind the Iron Curtain* (2023).